ST ERKENWALD

Saint Erkenwald (Middle English poem)

ST ERKENWALD

Edited by Ruth Morse

D.S.Brewer . Rowman and Littlefield

ⓒ Ruth Morse   1975

Published by D.S.Brewer Ltd
240 Hills Road, Cambridge, England
and by Rowman and Littlefield
81 Adams Drive, Totowa, New Jersey 07512, U.S.A.

ISBN 0 85991 009 1 (U.K.)

Library of Congress Cataloging in Publication Data

Saint Erkenwald (Middle English poem)
    St. Erkenwald.

    Bibliography: p.
    1. Erkenwald, Saint, Bp. of London, d. 693..Legends.
I. Morse, Ruth, ed.
PR1968.E4 1975   821'.1   75-2128
ISBN 0-87471-686-1

To DLM and GCM

PR
1968
E4
1975

Printed in Great Britain by
Redwood Burn Ltd, Trowbridge & Esher

ACKNOWLEDGMENTS

MANY PEOPLE HAVE helped me in the preparation of this edition. For stimulation and assistance of various kinds I am grateful to Dr.S.C.Aston, Prof.J.A.W.Bennett, Dr.D.S.Brewer, and Mr A.C.Spearing. Anyone who has worked in the University Library, Cambridge, will know what I owe to the staff, especially that of the old Anderson Room under the supervision of Mr George Stannard. At a later stage the Cambridge University Literary and Linguistic Computing Centre prepared a concordance and a series of indices which lightened the burden and increased the accuracy of the glossary. Prof. Robert Worth Frank, Jr. read an early draft of my Introduction. Mr Thorlac Turville-Petre saved me from a number of errors. Dr Helen Cooper has been a sympathetic and exacting critic throughout every stage of my work. A long-standing debit is recognized in the dedication. My husband, Stefan Collini, helped most of all.

RM

New Hall
Cambridge
June 1975

INTRODUCTION

'ST ERKENWALD' DESERVES to be considered as a poem of interest in its own right, rather than neglected as a dubious appendage to the brilliant poems usually attributed to the *Gawain*-poet, with which indeed it has some traditional relationship. It is generally agreed that it was composed in the late fourteenth century, roughly about the date of those poems. It was probably written in the light of, and perhaps soon after, the fuller version (B or C texts) of *Piers Plowman* (see below, Section III). An approximate date of 1400 may be suggested for its composition.

Three editions have appeared: Horstmann's in 1881, Gollancz's in 1922, and Savage's in 1926.[1] Only the first, which appeared in a large collection of legends, follows the arrangement of the manuscript. The two twentieth century editors, convinced that they were dealing with the work of the Gawain-poet, arranged the poem in quatrains, and concentrated their attention on sources and dialect; most subsequent studies have followed this pattern. Recently, the Gawain-poet's authorship has been questioned,[2] and in a variety of other ways the traditional interpretation has come to seem inadequate and the previous editions unsatisfactory.

For this edition I have transcribed the poem afresh from the unique manuscript in the British Museum in order to restore the original text in its original arrangement to the reader. In Section I of the Introduction I have provided a description of the Manuscript and a brief summary of the evidence bearing upon its date and composition. In Section II I have attempted to

---

1 Footnote references will be to author and year of publication. Full references will be found in the Bibliography.

2 Benson, 1965. For a discussion of the problem, see below.

establish what historical evidence relating to the life of Erkenwald would have been available to the author of the poem. It then becomes clear that he deliberately ignored much of this material, preferring to substitute certain familiar medieval themes, especially the famous legend of Gregory and Trajan. Section III, therefore, describes the uses of this and related motifs in other literature of the period, showing how it owed its importance to its bearing upon the problem of salvation. I have sketched the lineaments of the late fourteenth century theological debate upon this problem, and shown how, in the more familiar setting of *Piers Plowman*, it was treated as a literary subject. It is my contention that 'St.Erkenwald' was written as a contribution to this debate, and that it tells the story of the righteous heathen in a way that implies certain liberal theological interpretations of Good Works and their claim upon God's mercy. In Section IV I have considered the language and style of 'St.Erkenwald' in the light of recent discussion of the 'Alliterative Revival', and in Section V I have attempted to draw these various approaches together to provide a more satisfactory reading of the poem as a whole than has hitherto been suggested.

I

'ST.ERKENWALD' SURVIVES only in BM Ms.Harleian 2250, a collection consisting mainly of short selections copied from a variety of North West Midland sources. It is a paper folio, 29 x 20.5 centimeters, with watermark 'Tête de boeuf', bound in 1881.[3] If Horstmann, who used this

3 Briquet, 1907 (Vol.III, p.715) writes, 'La tête de boeuf est le plus abondant de tous les filigranes pour la période qui nous occupe, mais son usage ne s'est étendu que jusqu'aux dernières années du XVIe siècle.' Those marks which most resemble that found in the manuscript date from the second third of the fifteenth century and indicate that the paper was imported from

manuscript in his study of the *South English Legendary*, saw another binding, he makes no comment. The handwriting is Anglicana of the late fifteenth century with an admixture of secretary features. A detailed list of the contents will establish the context in which our poem is found, and will correct the descriptions to be found in the Harleian *Catalogue* (1808) and Carleton Brown's *Register*.

Items 1-18[4] are extracts from *The Stanzaic Life of Christ*.[5] This work is a compilation made in Chester in the fourteenth century from the *Legenda Aurea* and Higden's *Polychronicon*, Books I and IV. Higden, of course, was attached to St.Werburgh's Abbey in Chester, as the author of the *Stanzaic Life* may also have been. The poems are written in tetrameter quatrains. Foster rightly calls this a poor quality copy. The scribe has at several points practised the more formal Textura hand with decorated capitals in the margin, and drawn roses and geometric designs as well. Items 19, 24-32 (not 21-23 as Brown reports) are copies of a portion of the *South English Legendary*. They are lives of Saints Martin, John Baptist, Alban, Julian the Confessor, Julian the Hospitaller, three sections on the Cross, and Saints Quiriak and Helen. It is possible that the choice of these particular saints has some significance; if we knew more about the families and religious houses of fourteenth and fifteenth century Cheshire we might be able to discover either the model from which the excerpts were made or the man or men for whom they were selected. Item 20 is a long extract from *Speculum Christiani*,[6] a work which can be dated 1350-1400, possibly of

southern France. This shows that the assumption that the manuscript was copied around 1477 is correct.

4 I follow the Harleian *Catalogue* numeration.

5 Foster, 1926.

6 Holmstedt, 1933.

Lollard origin: tabulae 2 (on the Ten Commandments), 4
(on the Seven Deadly Sins), and 6 (Sayings of the Four
Philosophers). Holmstedt showed that the colophon to
this section is the signature of the scribe and the date
he finished copying. While the date, 1477, appears with-
in the box which the original scribe drew around the
colophon the name does not, and it is difficult to say
if the ink of the name matches the extract. The Thomas
Masse who signed his name here may or may not have been
the scribe. There was a large 'Massy' family in Cheshire
throughout the fifteenth century, and Thomas was a com-
mon Christian name, so no positive identification can be
made. Items 21, 22 are extracts from the Franciscan St.
Bonaventura's *Dieta Salutis*. Item 23 is 'St.Erkenwald'.
Our poem is one of the neatest transcriptions in the
manuscript. There are two two-line red initial capitals
at lines 1 and 177. A later hand glosses some difficult
words. Items 35-42 are extracts from Mirk's *Festial*.[7]
Mirk flourished in the early fifteenth century, so the
selections were composed over a considerable length of
time. The scribe seems to have had particular interest
in the *narratio* portions of the extracts he has copied,
and in several cases has copied only the *narratio*. This
may mean that the book was intended for a parish priest
or some person who had occasion to read the exemplary
stories aloud as part of his sermons. But the next few
items seem to indicate private use. They are an estimate
of the distance from the earth to the moon according to
Rabbi Moses (Item 33), a cure for fever (Item 34) and a
partial copy of a discourse on the Ten Commandments and
Vices and Virtues which may be a copy of the *Summa de
viciis et virtutibus* which was in the Franciscan convent
library at Chester.[8] The scribe left some blank pages at

7 Erbe, 1905.

8 This can be only conjecture until there is more study
  of these *Summae*. Francis, 1942, edited a *Book of Vices
  and Virtues* but did not examine all the manuscripts.

the end of this last Item (43), perhaps in order to go back and finish copying after an interruption. One of the blank pages was used later, possibly by the same person who glossed the difficult words in 'St.Erkenwald', to record a donation concerning Robert of Winchelsea, which I was unable to decipher, but this Item (44) is certainly not part of the original sequence.

The manuscript is thus composed of a variety of separate selections, many of them from works written at Chester. As it is written in a mixed hand, not a book hand, it may have been copied for private devotions. Several attempts have been made to identify the people who wrote their names in the manuscript in order to determine its provenance. Gollancz thought it probably belonged to Lawrence Booth, a West Country man with London connections— he was Dean of St.Paul's.[9] Foster identified Elsbyt Bothe with Elizabeth Booth, daughter of George Booth and wife to Richard Sutton.[10] C.A.Luttrell thought that the correct Booth family was the Barton, not the Dunham Massy, branch and that the manuscript originated somewhere in the triangle Chester-Eccles-Stockport.[11] He thought he had found the Thomas Bowker whose name appears in two places in the manuscript and identified him with the man who 'appears in Henry VIII's survey of 1535 as first cantarist at the chantry of Jesus and St.Mary the Virgin, founded at... Eccles'[12] but the available genealogies mention too many

9 Gollancz, 1922, pp.vi-vii.

10 Foster, 1926, p.xii. He refers to Ormerod's *Cheshire*, vol.I, p.402. There are in fact several Elizabeth Booths.

11 Luttrell, 1958, p.40.

12 *Ibid.*, p.40. If Luttrell has found the right Thomas Bowker it is significant that he is a priest of some wealth and influence who originally came from Chester, where he is mentioned in several local wills.

people with the same names to be sure of finding the right ones. It is not known who wrote 'per omnia secula seculo' (sic) on folio 79v, nor who was Neltho Norton (or Nettya Barton, as Luttrell reads it).[13] (There are no Nortons in the Cheshire *Visitations*.) All we can safely say is that the book probably originated in Cheshire, that it may have belonged to a member of the baronial family (or a branch thereof) of Booth, that it was copied in the late fifteenth century, that its dialect is Northwest Midlands.[14]

I have transcribed 'St Erkenwald' as it appears in the manuscript, with one division at line 177 where a red capital begins the line. I have silently expanded all normal abbreviations, brought capitalization into line with modern practice, and attempted to punctuate the poem to make it easier to read. While our text is obviously a copy (see 12. 94, 140) it is impossible to tell how many removes it is from the original.

II

THE EARLIEST MENTION of Erkenwald, Bishop of London, is Bede's brief biography in the *Ecclesiastical History*:[15]

Theodore then [after the Synod of 672/3] appointed Eorconwold bishop in London, for the East Saxons. Sebbi and Sighere, already mentioned, were the reigning monarchs. Both before and after his consecration, Eorconwold lived so holy a life that even now miracles bear witness to it. To this day the horse-litter

13 Luttrell, 1958, p.39.

14 On the dialect of the manuscript see the *Middle English Dictionary*; introductions to the poem by Gollancz and Savage; Oakden, 1930, 1935; Moore, Meech and Whitehall, 1935; M.S.Serjeantson, 1927. There is general agreement about the dialect of the manuscript.

15. B.Colgrave and R.A.B.Mynors, 1969, pp.354-7.

(feretrum eius caballarium) in which he used to be carried when ill is preserved by his followers and continues to cure many people afflicted with fevers and other complaints. Not only are people cured who are placed in or near the litter but splinters cut from it and taken to the sick bring speedy relief.

Before he was made Bishop, he founded two famous monasteries, one for himself and the other for his sister Aethelburgh, and established an excellent form of monastic Rule and discipline in both. His own was in the kingdom of Surrey near the river Thames at a place called Chertsey, that is, the isle of Ceorot. His sister's monastery he established at a place called Barking in the kingdom of the East Saxons [Essex] where she was to live as mother and nurse of a company of women devoted to God.

Erkenwald was consecrated Bishop of London in 675 or 676. He died in 693. Bede, who finished his Ecclesiastical History in 731,[16] is our best-placed witness; all later accounts depend on his. Bede did not include Erkenwald in his *Martyrology*, nor is Erkenwald to be found in any of the standard collections until the time of John of Tynemouth, and then, as one might expect, only in England.

For 450 years Erkenwald's shrine stood somewhere in the body of St.Paul's Cathedral. In 1148 (xviii Kal. Dec., or 14 Nov.) his remains were moved to the east side of the wall above the high altar; the second of St.Erkenwald's two feast days commemorates this translation (30 April, his main feast, is presumably the day of his death or burial). The shrine was sumptuous and renowned both for its magnificence and for miracles of healing. In the fourteenth century the saint became an instrument for the reform of the Cathedral clergy which Bishop Robert Braybrooke had begun in 1381. William Dugdale

16 Colgrave and Mynors, p.xix.

writes[17]

And in Anno MCCCLXXXVI (10 R 2./)/ *Robert Braybroke*
Bishop of *London*, by a solemn Decree ordaining, that
the days of the Conversion and *Commemoration* of Saint
Paul (to whom this Church was specially dedicated)
should be celebrated throughout his Diocese, equally
with the highest Festivalls, joyned therewith, the
day of the Buriall of this saint Erkenwald *viz. ult.
Aprilis*, and the day of his Translation, *viz. XVIII.
Kal. Dec. (cujus merita gloriosa in eadem Ecclesia
miraculose coruscant*, as saith the Instrument) which
had antiently been used to be kept holy, as he there
affirmeth; but of late neglected.

Bishop Braybrooke's appeals to ancient use were apparent
ly not as successful as he had hoped. In 1393 he again
commanded his clergy to attend service in the Cathedral
on the saint's feast days. Dugdale says that in 1533 the
Saint's body was spirited away; today there is no men-
tion of him anywhere in Wren's church.[18]
Besides this evidence there are two independent Latin
lives from the twelfth century which survive in five
manuscripts.[19] They are typical pious expansions of

17 William Dugdale, 1668, pp.20-22. He includes a sketch
of the shrine.

18 Modern biographies of Erkenwald can be found in *DNB*,
article by the Rev.William Hunt; in Stubbs's *Diction-
ary of Christian Biography* II, pp.177-9; in *Analecta
Bollandiana* (the most complete account) s.v. 30 April
in *April III*, pp.780-787.

19 Arcoid, nephew of Bishop Gilbert Universalis, who was
present at the translation, may have written the ver-
sion contained in Cot. Claud. A.5 (ff.135-8) and CCCC
161 (which also contains Miracles). Cott. Tiberius
E. 1 (ff.116b-122), a famous collection of Lives, and
Bodl. Tanner 15 and Lansdowne 436 contain a similar

14

suggestions in Bede, and borrowings from the numerous miracles of the corpus of legends. Miracles of Erkenwald and his equally saintly sister include their stretching a beam that was too short to hold up the roof of her convent. (See Appendix.) John of Tynemouth combined the two versions of the Life sometime in the first half of the fourteenth century. This is the version used by the Bollandists and followed by subsequent authorities. Dugdale printed the version in Cotton Claudius A.5; the other versions have never been printed.

Erkenwald is mentioned briefly in the English Chronicles: William of Malmesbury, *Gesta Pontificum Anglorum*; Matthew Paris, *Chronica Majora*; the *Flores Historiarum*. He still appears in the English Roman Catholic Breviary in the offices for 30 April. Far from being a shadowy name out of England's Anglo-Saxon past, Erkenwald was in the late Middle Ages an historically documented figure of some considerable importance in St.Paul's.

Yet the man who wrote 'St.Erkenwald', though he seems to have known something of the saint, sending him appropriately to Essex and placing him in the correct period, chose not to write of the miracles attributed to Erkenwald in any of the Lives, but to write something different. What he wrote, moreover, is not really a Saint's Life or Legend at all, although it apparently owes its survival to the assumption that it was. In Harley 2250, where 'St.Erkenwald' appears amidst a collection of Lives from the *South English Legendary*, *De Sancto Erkenwaldo* is obviously unlike the others. Besides its different style (it is the only piece written in alliterative long lines) it tells us nothing about Erkenwald's lineage, realization of vocation, mission, passion, death,

version. See T.D.Hardy, *Descriptive Catalogue of Materials*... vol.I, part I (London 1862) pp.293-295, for descriptions of the manuscripts and for the chronicles. John of Tynemouth's book, as revised by John Capgrave, was edited by Carl Horstmann, 1901.

15

posthumous miracles. It ignores the saint's idiosyncratic mode of transport— the obvious thing to have included.[20] We may go so far as to say that nothing in our poem need be attached to the Anglo-Saxon prince at all. As a legend excerpted from a longer Life it seems to make slightly more sense, but we are still left with the question of why the poet should have ignored all of the saint's own miracles and chosen an extraneous one which could be instantly identified with Trajan and Gregory.

This incident seems to have been the pious invention of the Monk of Whitby in his Life of St.Gregory.[21] It is,

20 The horse litter which belonged to Erkenwald was preserved in his shrine as a holy relic. It acquired the following miracle: Bishop Erkenwald, though afflicted with a painful swelling of his feet, would not allow sickness to interfere with his pastoral duties. In order to continue his Visitations, he had himself carried in a two-wheeled horse-cart. One day, while on a journey, one of the wheels fell off, but the cart, rather than cause any pain to the holy man, or delay him from his duties, continued to balance upon only one wheel. This kind of story is of a familiar type; it explains what is usually an emblematic illustration of the particular saint, e.g. the eastern pictures of St.George confronting the dragon that represents Sin inspiring the interpretation that he slew a dragon.

21 Gaston Paris, 1878, describes the development of the legend in great detail, and presents a convincing explanation for the connection with Trajan. The identification of the Erkenwald miracle with the Gregory-Trajan legend was made early. Loomis, 1920, thought the connection with Erkenwald was due to a pun rather than to anything to do with the actual content of the legend. Hulbert, 1919, showed that 'St.Erkenwald' was not adapted from Middle English poetry. Neither Gollancz, 1921, nor Savage, 1926, considered possible

16

on the surface at least, a simple story. While walking in the Forum one day Gregory is reminded of the Roman Emperor Trajan by the sight of Trajan's column. (In some more spectacular versions he opens the tomb underneath the column to find that Trajan's tongue has been preserved to talk to him. The monk who devised that presumably did not know that the Romans cremated their dead, but it would be naive to suppose that historical truth was the aim of such compilations.) Someone tells Gregory that Trajan, on the point of leaving Rome to go to war, was stopped by a widow who demanded justice for the murder of her son. Trajan held up his campaign long enough to deal with the case, even (again in more spectacular versions) discovering that the guilty man is his own son and sentencing him. Thus far the story of Trajan's justice is a commonplace. Just as Diocletian was throughout the Middle Ages known to have been a wicked Emperor to whom all persecutions of Christians were attributed, so Trajan was known to have been a just and good ruler. Now Gregory, impressed with Trajan, this just judge and righteous heathen, wept. God, impressed with Gregory's compassion, released Trajan from Hell, where he had been sent as an unbaptized pagan.

For 'St.Erkenwald' the scene is moved to Britain. Two motifs, suggested in the Gregory-Trajan legend, are expanded in our poem to emphasize its meaning. The good emperor becomes a Just Judge and the memory of Trajan becomes a miraculously preserved corpse.[22] Both motifs

reasons for the transfer of the legend. Only Chambers, 1923, suggested that there was some theological motive.

22 The Gregory-Trajan legend was also adapted for St.Patrick, but the Irish saint finds a giant left over from heroic days, and baptizes the giant upon the giant's own request. Despite a certain superficial resemblance, the Patrick- and Erkenwald- miracles are quite different, and Szöverffy is surely wrong to find the influence of Patrick on Erkenwald. See Szöverffy, 1956.

are familiar ones in Christian literature. Judges are a
constant concern throughout the Old Testament, partic-
ularly in the Prophets. They foreshadow Christ as Judge,
providing parallels both for the writers of the New
Testament and for the Christian writers who followed. A
judge who is just on earth imitates the divine judge and
has therefore a certain special sanctity. The miraculous
preservation of a corpse is also, at least outside the
special circumstances of Celtic literature, a similar
sign of sanctity. That the body of a holy man or woman
should resist corruption after death is a common belief.
It is to be met with outside specifically hagiographical
literature, where it is commonplace: in Dostoyevsky's
The Brothers Karamazov a scandal erupts because a holy
monk's corpse begins to putrefy sooner than was expected.
The Vita of St.Erkenwald presents us with the expected
miracle: nature is reversed and a sweet smell fills the
death chamber. Discoveries of miraculously preserved
corpses abounded throughout the Middle Ages, due perhaps
in no small measure to the competition for famous relics
to increase the importance of individual churches which
had to contain at least one holy relic in order to be
consecrated. St.Martin is a famous example. In the reign
of Henry II the monks of Glastonbury, who already claim-
ed the relics of Joseph of Arimathea, discovered two
miraculously preserved secular bodies in their church-
yard. The man was obviously a king, the woman lying be-
side him a queen— surely Arthur and Guinevere. Unfortun-
ately, a lecherous monk reached out to stroke the beauti-
ful blonde hair of the queen, and when he touched her
both bodies crumbled into dust— a fate that also befalls
our pagan judge in the poem, 11.342-4. There is thus a
precedent for the poet's story; a pagan judge underneath
St.Paul's would have seemed quite plausible to his
audience. The Erkenwald-poet could count on his audi-
ence's expectation of some kind of miracle of God's
grace from the moment that he mentioned the discovery of
a perfectly preserved corpse.

18

III

THE GREGORY-TRAJAN LEGEND was widely known in medieval Europe, and was widely used to refer to the problem of the salvation of the righteous heathen. Dante, adapting the story as he found it in the *Fiore di filosofi*, which in turn adapted the legend as found in the *Speculum historiale* of Vincent of Beauvais, mentions Trajan and Gregory both in the *Purgatorio* and the *Paradiso*. In *Purgatorio* X 73-96 Dante the character sees the picture of Gregory's 'great victory' painted on a wall and hears how Trajan humbled himself to help the poor widow. In the *Paradiso* Trajan is discovered to be one of two heathens who occupy exalted places in heaven. Canto XIX opens Dante's discussion of salvation of the righteous heathen; ll. 79-90 presents the obvious difficulties. In the next Canto, Dante makes his opinion quite clear. In XX 43-8 and 106-17 he refers to the salvation of Trajan as proof of God's mercy and justice. From the time of Dante's earliest commentators his purpose was recognized.23

In England, Gregory and Trajan appear as an example of the importance of just and good works in the *Policraticus* of John of Salisbury. Like Dante, John tells the story of Trajan's encounter with the widow, then goes on to draw his conclusions.24 In the *Legenda Aurea* Voragine

---

23 Benevenuto writes, in the midst of his long discussion of the problem of the salvation of the righteous heathen, 'Breviter ergo vult dicere ex iste fictione talem conclusionem, quod talis vir paganus, de cuius salvatione non sperebatur, est salvabilis.' (On Canto XX) J.P.Lacaito, ed.: Benevenuto de Rambaldis de Imola Comentum super Dantis Alighieris Comoedium (Florence, 1887) vol.v. p.263.

24 Webb, 1909, I, pp.317-18. 'Vnde merito praefertur aliis cuius virtus prae ceteris ita sanctis placuit ut eorum meritis solus sit liberatus.' (*Policraticus* V, 560a).

begins likewise with the emperor's just act.[25] He goes on to give as many variants and opinions on what Gregory did and how he did it as he could find. Voragine has obviously been through the literature on the subject.

What looks like a relatively straightforward miracle of intercession had in fact become the crucial text in numerous discussions, because it embodies contradictions difficult to reconcile. If Trajan was in Hell, where men are committed forever, how could he be saved? If, as was indubitably true, the sacrament of Baptism was necessary for Salvation, how could an unbaptized heathen ascend to heaven? Did Gregory presume to question God's decision to damn Trajan? If Trajan could be saved without the machinery of the Church, did that not threaten her claim to hold the keys to eternal life? To theologians the most important question was that essential one about the power (*potentia*) of God: is God free to contradict his own ordinances?

One reaction to the problems raised by the Gregory-Trajan legend was to re-write the legend. The truth of the whole legend was not questioned; the reviser simply rewrote, or 'restored', the ending that 'ought' to have been there. This is an attitude to historical writing that strikes us as the very opposite of history, but was in accord with medieval ideas about historical truth, as seen, for example, in Laʒamon's adaptation of Wace's adaptation of Geoffrey's *Historia Regum Brittanniae*; there was no reason to doubt that Laʒamon's main points were true. Revisers of the miracle had Gregory punished for using his saintly power to release a pagan: given the choice between lingering sickness until his death or three days in Purgatory after it, he chose sickness.

25 Graesse, 1850, Cap. XLVI, pp.196-7. Voragine's sources are discussed by Paris, 1878. The *Legenda Aurea* was extremely popular in England, translated in 1348 and later again by Caxton, who added a Life of St.Erkenwald which he abridged from Capgrave.

20

Some versions question whether Gregory actually prayed for Trajan, or whether it was simply the sight of his compassion that moved God. This would absolve the saint of any charge of presumption. Or, it was thought that perhaps Gregory's intercession achieved only the deferment of Trajan's punishment until the Day of Judgement. This, however, hardly seemed worthwhile, and again, the body of the legend contradicted this interpretation. Thomas Aquinas was at one point ready to accept this possibility, but at the same time suggests the solution that Trajan had not been damned eternally.[26] Guillaume d'Auxerre, the early thirteenth century theologian, author of the *Summa Aurea*, preferred the version used by Dante: Gregory called Trajan back into life. Thus, afforded a moment in which to experience baptism, Trajan could indeed be saved. This is the type of solution adopted by the Erkenwald-poet, though I do not suggest by this that he knew Guillaume's or Dante's works. The report in the *Legenda Aurea* would suffice.

The other reaction to the story of Gregory and Trajan was to reinterpret the theology of salvation. Salvation comes as a gift of Grace from God to the man who believes faithfully, and Baptism is the sacrament which marks that Grace. Since the remission of sin is achieved by Baptism, Baptism is therefore obviously necessary for salvation. Problems immediately present themselves, and the scholastic philosophers were not slow to notice them. What kind of gift is Salvation— can it be earned, i.e. merited? How much and what must a man believe? What possibility of salvation is there for the man who is ignorant of Christ, who, like Trajan and the pagan judge in 'St.Erkenwald', have not been baptized? While accepting

---

26 Aquinas returned to Trajan several times in his writings. In *Summa Theologica* III Suppl.q 71 art 5 he accepts the miracle on the authority of St.John Damascene but weighs several possibilities to explain what happened and how it could be.

that Grace is a great mystery and that the Spirit blows where it will, men still speculated about what laws, if any, God had ordained. In the twelfth century theologians like Hugh of St.Victor and St.Bernard of Clairvaux set a sort of 'minimum requirement' for salvation. Men must believe in God and in his providence; they must believe in a Mediator. The pagan judge in 'St.Erkenwald' meets these requirements (11.284, 298); Trajan did not— our poet has added them.

When in the thirteenth century, Aquinas put his imprimatur on the rather vague formulation of belief he emphasized the necessity of Baptism, in order to account for the salvation of those, for example the martyrs, who had apparently not been baptized with water, he extended the definition. This is provided for in the commentary on Mark 16: 15-16. Jesus appears to his disciples after the Crucifixion and says

Euntes in mundum universum praedicate evangeliam omni creaturae. Qui crediderit, et baptizatus fuerit, salvus erit: qui vero non crediderit, condemnabitur.

Go forth to every part of the world, and proclaim the Good News to the whole creation. Those who believe it and receive baptism will find salvation; those who do not believe will be condemned.

(New English Bible.)

Nicholas de Lyra's gloss is typical: '*Qui crediderit*, et iuxta praescriptum vitam instituerit, *et baptizatus fuerit* baptismo vel fluminus, vel flaminis, vel sanguinis, saluus erit...' Aquinas follows this three-fold interpretation: besides *Baptismus acquae* (*fluminus*) which is the normal form of baptism, there is also *Baptismus sanguinus*, the blood of martyrdom which repeats the sacrifice of blood on the Cross, and *Baptismus flaminis*, the most difficult of the three to comprehend, as it seems to be a convenient escape route when the other two are obviously lacking. Based on the moment when the Holy Ghost descended on the disciples at Pentecost, it

22

involves the understanding of *flaminis* as 'of the Holy Ghost', also interpreted as 'firm belief' (as the sin against the Holy Ghost, the one sin that cannot be forgiven, is despair, that is, refusal to believe). St. Thomas wrote[27]

> Baptism of water has its efficacy from Christ's Passion, to which a man is conformed by Baptism, and also from the Holy Ghost, as first cause. Now although the effect depends on the cause, the cause far surpasses the effect, nor does it depend on it. Consequently, a man may, without Baptism of water, receive the Sacramental effect of Christ's passion, in so far as he is conformed to Christ by suffering for Him... In like manner, a man receives the effect of Baptism by the power of the Holy Ghost, not only without Baptism of water, but also without Baptism of Blood, forasmuch as his heart is moved by the Holy Ghost to believe in and love God and to repent of his sins: wherefore this is also called Baptism of Repentance... Thus, therefore, each of these Baptisms is called Baptism, forasmuch as it takes the place of Baptism. [Aquinas then goes on to cite the case of the Good Thief.] And also 'The sacrament of Baptism may be wanting to anyone in reality but not in desire... And such a man can obtain salvation without being actually baptized, on account of his desire for Baptism...'[28]

Thus it is that Trajan could be saved, though the difficulty still remains that the only mark of his *baptismus flaminis* is the legend's statement that he went to heaven. The original writer wrote what seemed appropriate to him. The theologians had to try to explain how the apparently impossible might occur.

27 Dominican trans. 1914, pp.119-21 *Summa Theologica* III q.LXVI a.11 (not art.2) quoted by T.P.Dunning, 1943, p.52.

28 *Summa Theologica* III q.LXVIII art.2. (p.143).

In the fourteenth century conflicting explanations led to controversy, condemnations, and charges of heresy. Scholars are not yet in accord over the complex debate on the question of salvation. Enough can be said, however, to provide a context for 'St.Erkenwald'. Along with the question of whether or not a man could merit salvation came the problem of predestination and free will: if God knows who is to be saved, then does it follow that the issue has been decided long before a man's actions could be judged? If this be the case, can a man be considered free at all? We shall not follow the debate through to the logical conclusions about pre-destination and double predestination. Let it suffice to say that Duns Scotus's treatment of such questions as these was followed by those of Occam, Gregory of Rimini, and many other Oxford and Paris theologians, among whom, at the end of the century, Wyclif was prominent. Thomas Bradwardine's *De Causa Dei Contra Pelagium* was a part-icularly famous document in the debate, embodying as it did a rather extreme limitation of man's power to act without divine aid. The 'Modern Pelagians' Bradwardine opposed were such men as Occam and his followers who ex-tolled man's free will and ability to merit grace in their scheme of salvation, thus limiting God's power. Chaunticleer mentions Bradwardine in his discussion of predestination together with St.Augustine and Boethius in the 'Nun's Priest's Tale'— surely a sign that the subject and its controversialists were well-known at the end of the century.

What is of particular importance to us is that Brad-wardine opposed any suggestion that man might merit grace. The idea that men had a disposition to do good of their own free will, which had been accepted by St. Thomas and other scholastics,[29] was to Bradwardine the great error of the age. He spent long pages denying that

29 Leff, 1957, pp.74-5.

24

man's good works have any claim on God's grace.[30] 'Brad-
wardine's position, in fact, amounts to a complete re-
jection of merit as a human achievement.'[31] Though he
quotes Hugh of St.Victor, St.Bernard and St.Thomas[32] he
has gone far beyond their carefully balanced syntheses
of faith and reason, to a position strikingly like that
which Luther was to take. 'Faith alone can make us just-
ified: works have no part to play in achieving that
which comes from Him alone.' 'Sequuntur enim opera iust-
ificatum, non praecedunt iustificandum, sed sola fide
sine operibus praecedentibus sit homo iustus.'[33] A man
without faith, that is, an infidel, *could not* be right-
eous, since there could be no righteousness without
grace: 'ubi fides non erat bonus opus non erat.'[34] The
man who wrote these words rose to be Archbishop of Cant-
erbury; his influence, reputation, and authority had all
the weight of that office, however briefly held, behind
it. Bradwardine's position is provocative of despair: he
denies man any participation in his own salvation. He
was bound to evoke strong reactions, and among the writ-
ers who stressed man's hope in salvation through good
works were Will Langland and the author of 'St.Erkenwald'.

Langland is a particularly important author for read-
ers of 'St.Erkenwald', because *Piers Plowman* is, with
the *Legenda Aurea*, the most likely place where our poet
could have read the Trajan-Gregory legend. Langland
follows the treatment in the Latin, and sets out the
theological crux. This problem of salvation, predestina-

---

30 *'Predestination does not happen on account of human
   works, but on account of the gracious will of God.'*
   Oberman, 1957, p.115 (his italics).

31 Leff, 1957, p.78.

32 *ibid.*, p.113.

33 *ibid.*, p.83 and n.

34 *ibid.*, p.155 and n.

tion and free will is one of the continuing themes of
Piers Plowman, and the theological issues have been ex-
plored in relation to Langland by a succession of schol-
ars.[35] We will conclude our survey of uses of the Greg-
ory-Trajan legend with a somewhat detailed look at *Piers*
because of the resemblances between it and 'St.Erken-
wald'. The problem comes to a head in Passus XI of the
A-text. The B-text expands it (Passus X-XII) at some
length, and the B-text version is thoroughly and care-
fully revised for the C-text. I shall avoid the many
complications which arise from the three versions, and
concentrate on Langland's treatment of the Gregory-
Trajan legend, which does not differ much between B- and
C-texts.

In B XI Will is trying to find out exactly what in-
sures salvation. Men must believe loyally, but learning
alone will not guarantee it, baptism alone will not as-
sure it— though Will tries the suggestion that everyone
who is baptized must be saved. Baptism must be preceded
by contrition. Into the midst of the learned debate (it
is written in imitation of scholastic disputation) Lang-
land introduces what we can now recognise to be the
usual contradictory example, Trajan, who is ready to up-
set any theory Will might have been about to propound.

'ȝee! baw for bokes!' quod one . was broken oute of
    helle,
Hiȝte *Troianus*, had ben a trewe knyȝte . toke witnesse
    at a pope,
How he was ded and dampned . to dwellen in pyne,
For an vncristene creature; . '—clerkis wyten the sothe,

---

35 The relation between *Piers* and the *Legenda Aurea* is
   noticed by Dunning, 1943, p.53. See also Frank, 1957;
   Hort, n.d.; and G.H.Russell, 1966. R.W.Chambers re-
   cognized the existence of the theme in 1923, but did
   not realize that the debate was still an open one,
   and that Langland's theology was indeed orthodox.

That al the clergye vnder Cryste . ne miȝte me cracche
    fro helle,
Bot onliche loue and leaute . and my lawful domes.

(B XI 135-40)

C is more specific than B in making it quite clear that
Trajan was saved because of his 'Loue, withoute leel by-
leyve . and [his] lawe ryghtful' (CXIII. 86). Love is
the generalized *caritas* which Langland emphasizes
throughout the whole poem. Love, loyalty, faith, and
good works have contradictory claims. While no one of
these values will assure man of salvation, neither will
the lack of any one of them lead to his damnation, as
Ymagynatyf makes clear in Passus XII (B). We are reminded,
as elsewhere in *Piers Plowman*, that 'grace is a gyfte of
god . and of grete loue spryngeth' (B XII 70, and simil-
arly in C XV 35ff).[36] God will save whom he chooses, and
yet some knowledge of church doctrine is a help in the
struggle for salvation: there are many ways to merit
bliss. The Good Thief, who, despite his evil life, was
saved because he believed, is twice juxtaposed with Tra-
jan, who, despite his lack of belief, was saved because
of his justice.[37]

    Clergye, ne kynde witte . ne knew neuere the cause,
    Ac Kynde [God] knoweth the cause hym-selue . and no
        creature elles.

(B XII 225-6, expanded in C XV 156-61)

It is an old answer: who is man to question the justice
of God?
    Ymagynatyf has another answer, similar to that offer-
ed by St.Thomas.

    Troianus was a trewe knyȝte . and toke neuere Cristen-
        dome,

36 Parallel passages are quoted from Skeat's edition of
    the three texts, 1886.

37 The Good Thief is also one of Aquinas' examples.

And he is sauf, so seith the boke [*Legenda Sanctorum*]
. and his soule in heuene.
For there is fullyng of fonte . and fullyng in blode-
shedynge,
And thorugh fuire is fullyng . and that is ferme bileue
Adveni+ ignis diuinus, non comburens, sed illuminans,
etc.
Ac trewth that trespassed neuere . ne transuersed
aȝeines his lawe,
But lyueth as his lawe techeth . and leueth there be
no bettere,
And if there were, he wolde amende . and in suche will
deyeth,
Ne wolde neuere trewe god . but treuth were allowed;
And where it worth or worth nouȝt . the bileue is
grete of treuth,
And an hope hengyng ther-inne . to have a mede for his
treuthe.

(B XII 280-9, C XV 205-17)

The C-text is even more emphatic. After line 288 of B we
find

And hope hongeth ay ther-on . to haue that treuthe
deserueth
Quia super pauca fidelis fuisti, supra multa te con-
stituam:
And that is loue and large huyre . yf the lord be
trewe,
And cortesie more than couenant was . what so clerkes
carpen;
For al worth as god wole '— . and ther-with he
vanshede.

(C XV 214-17)

The Passus and the Dream end on this strong note. Lang-
land seems to want to say, via his many voices, that
while salvation and grace are a mystery, it is still
possible to merit God's free gift by good works. The
Erkenwald-poet's theology is similar. His God 'þat riȝt

28

euer alowes, / And loues al þe lawes lely þat longen to trouthe / ...most...menskes men for mynnyng of riʒtes' (267-70). After Bradwardine's general condemnation of the efficacy of human effort, Langland and the Erkenwald-poet offer some comfort.

It should now be obvious that there is a theological problem that was widely discussed both in the scholarly literature of the fourteenth century, and in the imaginative literature of the vernacular. The intercessive miracle which saved Trajan from Hell led to a more abstract concern with the general problem of salvation, in which Trajan himself became the symbol of a knotty dilemma. If we look at other poems in which the problem of salvation appears, the close resemblance of *Piers Plowman* and 'St.Erkenwald' seems the more striking. If we look at a brief quotation from 'Death and Liffe' the difference will be obvious:

> If yee [loue] well the L[ord] þat light in the mayden,
> & be christened with creame & in your creed beleue,
> Haue no doubt of yonder Death, my deare children...
>
> (ll. 436-8)[38]

This is nothing like the seeking after a solution to the problem of salvation. There is nothing here of 'fullyng' or 'trewth', 'allow-ing' or 'law', the resemblances of terminology that exist between *Piers* and 'St.Erkenwald'.

Neither the manuscript in which the poem is found nor our scanty knowledge of the area in which it was written (if it was composed in the same dialect as appears in the manuscript) give us any hint as to why the poet wrote what he did. His purpose may have been simply to provide an exemplum of God's infinite mercy— though in that case he has certainly taken extraordinary pains to make his point. The verbal resemblances to *Piers Plowman* may simply be the result of two poets of the alliterative school writing about the same subject. Perhaps

38 Gollancz, 1930.

29

there is some relationship between *Piers* and 'St.Erken-
wald', as there seems to be between *Piers* and, say, 'Mum
and Sothsegger'. It is likely that there was, in the
late fourteenth century, vernacular writing about the
salvation controversy that had earlier occupied scholas-
tic philosophers writing in Latin. The context of the
theological debate certainly explains 'St.Erkenwald'
better than any generic label.

Duns Scotus, William of Occam, and Adam of Woodham
had developed the heterodox 'assumption that man can act
in such a way that God can regard what he has done as
worthy of reward or as equivalent to that which could
have been wrought by grace: or put more simply, that man
can act morally even when not in grace.'[39] Our poet is
more orthodox: he makes the bishop repeat the whole bap-
tismal formula, thus avoiding one of the difficulties of
the Gregory-Trajan legend. While accepting the claim im-
plicit in the pagan's good works, the poet withholds
salvation until the Grace of God is formally awarded
through a *Baptismus aquae*. The poet was making a claim
for the salvation of the righteous heathen within the
complicated but widely known context of the claim of
merit upon salvation. Perhaps the poet was trying to re-
concile the problems posed by *potentia absoluta* and
potentia ordinata: while God could have saved the pagan
without the infusion of Grace (because God can do any-
thing He likes), in fact the miracle occurs so that sal-
vation comes in accordance with God's ordinances (the
Divine laws which govern the universe).

This new explanation raises with it a new question.
Why did the poet attach the miracle to Erkenwald, fourth
bishop of London? The whole poem has been carefully con-
structed to look like an historical event, with its use
of what was then respectable history. Erkenwald's exist-
ence is vouched for by Bede, an unimpeachable source,
who provides the story of Augustine's struggles to

39 Leff, 1961, p.182.

30

establish Roman Christianity in Britain and who records
the names and careers of Augustine's Anglo-Saxon heirs.
The judge, too, is carefully placed in an historical
context, this time provided by Geoffrey of Monmouth,
perhaps via the English version by Laȝamon. The whole
city of London, that great capital, is called to witness
the poet's miracle. Surely his insistence on that wit-
ness is part of his claim that the miracle is to be taken
seriously. It really happened, and was seen by all the
people of London and many important people from else-
where in Britain. More, the 'confirming of the Christian
faith' which is the purpose of the miracle, was also a
message of comfort about the kind of faith the poet's
audience was to have, because the miracle proves the
efficacy of good works, and reminds man of his privilege
of hope in his own ability to do good and merit salva-
tion. Who could doubt a miracle so well documented and
witnessed?

IV

'ST.ERKENWALD' IS one of the poems of the so-called
'Alliterative Revival'.[40] It follows the typical pattern
of four stresses with medial caesura, normally alliter-
ates aa/ax, and draws upon the rich stock of formulae of
the alliterative poetic vocabulary. The poet uses the
alliterative style with great variety and purpose. He
changes the alliterative pattern or rhythm of a line
according to the events described (unlike, for example,
the author of *The Destruction of Troy*, who used the aa/
ax pattern over 90% of the time) and exploits the possib-
ilities of alliteration for rhetorical purposes (unlike
the author of the *Morte Arthure*, whose long series of

40 On the 'Alliterative Revival' see the articles listed
   in the Bibliography by J.R.Hulbert and Elizabeth Salt-
   er. There is no single book-length study except the
   two-volume survey by Oakden, 1930, 1935, now very
   much out of date.

lines alliterating on the same sound exemplify mere technical virtuosity).

The first line of the poem is a good example of the 'normal' line (notice that the alliterating letter need not begin a word). This is the rhythmic and alliterative structure the poet uses to narrate or describe. The lines are paratactic, compounded rather than joined in long complex sentences, which might be difficult for an audience to assimilate. Often, long series of end-stopped lines are organized in parallel pairs, which are probably what led Gollancz and Savage to believe that the poem was written in quatrains. The poet was not ruled by a verse form, however; he made his syntax order his material. When he wants to tell us what Augustine did when he came to England, he uses three pairs of lines to do it, rather like a six-line paragraph (11.13-18). When this fast moving norm is interrrupted it is often to convey more important information or to change the tone. A rhythmic variation forces a change in the reader's handling of the line, and the audience hears the beginning of a new paragraph. An early example of this comes in 1.46, when the workmen discover the tomb,

>þai founden fourmyt on a flore a ferly faire toumbe.
>
>(aaa/aax)

Here the extra alliteration is accented by the extra stress. This paratactic construction lends itself to dramatic pauses, as in the moment when the bishop turns from celebrating mass to confront the corpse. The poet calls our attention to the lords who 'ply' to Erkenwald by inserting them parenthetically, and the extended half-line (as above, 1.46) adds emphasis.

The alliteration need not be underscored by rhythmic variation, such as an extended half-line, in order to indicate a change. There are twenty-two examples of the same alliteration appearing in two consecutive lines, and one example of three consecutive lines.[41] This ornate alliteration seems to be used to indicate a higher style, as may be seen by comparing the first hundred

lines of the poem (four examples) which are straighfor-
ward narration, with the Dean's thirteen-line summary of
the preceding narration (two two-line consecutive allit-
erations, but in fact the alliteration is denser than
this indicates, because all four lines alliterate on 'l',
and there are two more separate 'l'-lines in the speech
as well, two separate lines on 'k', two 'm', and inter-
nal words in non-stressed and non-alliterating positions
which add more instances of these three sounds). Ornate
alliteration also appears in the Bishop's first speech
to the corpse, where we find three two-line consecutive
alliterations in ten lines, and one instance of inter-
locking alliteration, that is, the last stressed word,
which is non-alliterating (aa/ax), of one line, becomes
the alliterating sound of the following line. The judge's
speeches are less ornate; perhaps because they are long-
er they tend to be organized in the parallel-type con-
struction noted above.

One place in the poem contains most of these effects
within a short space. In lines 265-284 the rhythmical
variations are complemented by three two-line and one
three-line consecutive alliteration, and four separate
lines on 'r' and two on 'l'. This passage is central to
the poem, and is appropriately the place where most
rhetorical heightening is displayed.

41 In 11.26f, 67f, 82f, 92f, 105f, 111f, 116f, 146f, 149f,
   178f, 181f, 184f?, 193f, 213f, 230f, 260f, 269f, 273f,
   283f, 326f, 331f, 341f, and 314-16. Oakden found only
   sixteen two-line and one three-line examples of con-
   secutive alliteration, though he was using Gollancz's
   emended text which should have increased the number
   of examples. This count does not consider other, more
   complex alliterative effects, like the non-alliterat-
   ing syllable of one line becoming the alliterating
   sound of the next, or internal, non-stressed alliter-
   ation, because it is not clear how far these were
   conscious devices.

V

WE MAY NOW, after this long prolegomenon, consider 'St. Erkenwald' in the light of its intellectual and poetical context.[42]

The first thirty-two lines of the poem form an historical prologue, in which time, places, protagonist, and theme are introduced. In terms of the narrator's art the near-present 'At London in Englond noȝt full long sythen' soon stretches backward in time to create an immediate situation (the establishment or re-establishment of the true faith) which is yet fluid enough to encompass pre-Saxon Britain and almost contemporary Britain. This wide interpretation is supported by the series of digressive recapitulations of English history, whose relevance to the theme will only later become obvious. Names are introduced in these first lines as parts of similar patterns, e.g. the mention of St.Erkenwald leads to the fact that in his time the church was rebuilt (and implied in rededication is the idea of spiritual renewal), and then we are led to Hengist and what the Saxons did (which will also explain how a pre-Saxon judge came to be buried in St.Paul's), and then St.Austyn comes and transforms the London churches— bringing us back to the establishment of the faith. The importance of this cleansing and rededication is emphasized by repetition in the grammatical structure. The poet also uses tense changes (1.33 from past to present for three lines to bring us up to the events the poem narrates) to emphasize the links with the past (1.36), for the relationships between past and present run throughout the poem.

The workmen are in the process of checking the foundations of the Cathedral (a physical establishing) when

42 Two articles present helpful readings of 'St.Erkenwald': Petronella, 1967, and McAlindon, 1970, but neither takes fully into account the theological controversy and the alliterative tradition. McAlindon, moreover, is misled by Gollancz's emendations.

they find a relict of the past in the shape of a marvel-
lous tomb. When they open the tomb at the command of the
mayor they find a most unusual corpse inside. Far from
showing any signs of decay, it looks more like the body
of a man who has just fallen into a deep sleep: the
judge will be called from sleep to waking, from death to
life, from damnation to salvation. The parallel movement
is well under way. There are what look like explanatory
letters carved into the tomb, but nobody can read them;
rumours spread quickly and disrupt the usual life of the
town, so Erkenwald is sent for to solve the mystery. The
bishop is a good shepherd who has gone on a visitation
of one of the religious houses in his care.[43] When he
returns he avoids both the crowds which come to meet him
and the corpse itself; he shuts the doors behind him and
spends the night in vigil and meditation, praying for
the grace to understand the marvel 'in confirmyng þi
Cristen faith'. And between the ringing of day bell and
dawn he receives assurances that he will know. The com-
mon alliterative phrase 'day over drof' has been handled
in a slightly different way. The poet has reversed the
usual order, by making day supersede night rather than
vice versa; by slightly lengthening the first half-line
he emphasizes the passing of the long night. 'þe darke
nyȝt ouer drofe & day belle ronge' (1.117). It is in
such slight variations as this that the subtlety of the
alliterative formulaic style lies. The suggestion (1.118)
that he has risen early is modified by the explanation
that the reason he was awake before dawn was because he
had been up all night praying.

The people of London have none of the Bishop's assur-
ance. They are kept continually before us by apparently
casual references to them throughout the poem. When Er-

43 We are told that he is in Essex, where the historical
   Erkenwald's Barking house was located. This suggests
   that the poet had some acquaintance with the litera-
   ture about the saint.

kenwald celebrates mass in the presence of all the
people, his congregation is not merely composed of the
diverse inhabitants of London, but of representatives
from all over England (11.134-5). The solemnity of the
occasion is marked by specifying that it is a high mass,
a Votive mass chosen especially for this occasion (see
Note to 1.132). The bishop is assisted by his ministers
and the Cathedral choir, and he is surrounded by the
highest people of the land when he steps down from the
altar and crosses the church to the marvellous tomb.
Still dressed in his episcopal robes, as high priest of
God, he will be in the appropriate state, temporal and
spiritual, to baptize the pagan judge in the presence of
the congregation.

The Dean, pointing with one finger, summarizes the
events and reaches the conclusion that this body, which
no one can identify, must have been preserved by a
marvel. It is important that the Dean's interpretation
should be both inadequate and wrong, as it provides the
opportunity for the bishop to make the point that man's
reason alone is insufficient. This would have been an
instantly recognizable theological point; however much
the poet is emphasizing the dignity and worth of man, he
is also aware of the majesty and glory of God. Just as,
in the prologue, one word led to the outline of a larger
situation, so here the poet links the bishop's first
speech to a word which has immediately preceded it. He
emphasizes the power of God to work a miracle (11.163-5)
as if he were teaching and persuading his audience, and
asserts the nature of the relationship between creatures
and creator: man is weak, his reason cannot comprehend
God's might, but God will help those who call on him. It
is the same kind of 'middle route' the poet takes on the
issue of salvation. The bishop predicts the miracle on
the people's acceptance of and participation in his
faith.

  Bot glow we all opon Godde and His grace aske,
  þat careless is of counsell and comforthe to sende,

And þat in fastynge of ȝour faith and of fyne bileue,
I shal auay ȝow so verrayly of vertues His
þat ȝe may leue vpon long þat he is Lord myȝty
And fayne ȝour talent to fulfille if ȝe hym frende leues.
(11.171-6)

This is the end of the first section of the poem, a
rhetorically strong position. One reason for the pagan's
preservation is implicit in the present situation, in
which the people of the newly redeemed community need
miraculous confirmation of their belief. This also ex-
plains why the pagan was left behind at the Harrowing of
Hell— not for his own sake but for the sake of others.

The second section of the poem begins exactly half
way through. The bishop 'turnes to þe toumbe and talkes
to þe corce'. The corpse speaks, explicitly recognizing
the power of God by which Erkenwald has commanded it,
and reveals itself to have been a Just Judge who consist-
ently followed the dictates of Truth (as, of course, he
saw it). He fulfills all but one of the necessary qual-
ifications for salvation: he is contrite and humble (11.
198, 211, 283-4), believes in God and God's Providence
(11.195-6, 267-72, 283-92, etc.), and in Christ as
Mediator and Saviour (11.289-99). The separation of body
and soul, familiar from English and Latin debate litera-
ture, overcomes one of the difficulties of the Trajan
legend: the judge's body is called back into life while
his soul remains in Limbo. The motif of the preservation
of an uncorrupted body— which all the people, including
the Dean, assume to be the miracle— has the striking and
yet recognizable variation that the totally preserved
(holy) man is a pagan. The poet has improved on his
source to create what must have been great tension for a
medieval audience.

That the poet thought that the pagan deserved salva-
tion is apparent from the way he has written the judge's
speeches. Though the judge himself is ostensibly too
humble to claim God's mercy as of right, the poet makes
him make his case, using such legal terms that we may

37

see the pagan making a quasi-legal 'plea' for salvation (11.188, 201, 232, 267 and see Notes to these lines). The legal terminology is more than a literary metaphor, more than language appropriate to its speaker: it was an accepted aspect of understanding God's absolute freedom and His movement from *misericordia* to *iustitia*. There is a divine order in which, though we can hardly understand it, natural law exists, and to which God has freely committed himself.[44]

Erkenwald, moved by the judge's recital, expresses a wish (not a prayer) that he might baptize him and thereby save him. Dramatically this is the weakest point in the poem for us, however crucial theologically, for Erkenwald pronounces the whole baptismal formula where we might expect him to send someone for water. The single tear which the bishop sheds on the judge's face in combination with the words of the baptism Erkenwald wishes to give suffice to raise the soul of the pagan from Limbo to Heaven, where he is instantly welcomed to the sacred feast. The poet overcomes a potentially anticlimactic dénouement (the events the corpse narrates are already in the past for him but must be explained for the benefit of those who live under temporal time) and even exploits a difficult situation to stress the instantaneous virtue of baptism. The transitions are again reflected in the poet's tense changes, which are not merely an idiosyncracy of the alliterative form, but follow the sense of the narration, beginning with that excellent signal in 1.324, '*Oure* sauyoure be louyd,' which contrasts with the pagan's previous '*ȝour* Criste' (1.209) and tells us everything in one word. The judge's plaint is in the present tense when he describes his situation, changes to the past to describe the historical events of the Fall and the Harrowing of Hell, and back to the present again, and the bishop's answer is in

44 See H.Oberman, 1967; Leff, 1957, where he attributes the opinion to Duns; and Leff, 1961, chapter V.

the past tense. The judge's present after his salvation is the timeless one of heavenly bliss, and the people's present is already his past when he explains it. The Londoners remain in historical time, which reclaims the miraculously preserved body in a moment's dissolution which is narrated in the past tense, but reflected on, by the poet and not in the dialogue, in the present tense as a timeless truth. It is a splended touch that salvation is immediately followed by bodily dissolution: everyone had thought that the preservation of the 'ferly' was the miracle, but the true miracle was the salvation of the heathen, to which the wonder was the means. And where the movement of the metaphors of the poem have been from darkness to light, here at the culminating moment the shining body is pulverized as we watch. The poet finishes his tale in a remarkably brief four line conclusion. Now the mass is ended, in mourning and mirth (a return to the upward motion of the poem) for the death which is redeemed by eternal life, and the people file out of the church to a spontaneously miraculous re-cessional— the sudden ringing of church bells.

The crowd is a most important 'character' in 'St.Er-kenwald', and the poet has spent many lines telling us about its composition and behaviour. The first mention of the corporate 'people' comes in the prologue, when the Saxons came (11.9-10). 'The people' are the primary audience for the confirming of Christianity; they in-clude the masons at work on St.Paul's (11.39-41), the various clergy who serve there, and the inhabitants of the town in all their estates (59-67, 134-5, 142-5). All the world has come to watch this miracle. Their react-ions, even their voices, are recorded for us, from the initial wonder, to the attempts to identify the body and the inability to recall any legend about the tomb, which has been punctuated in the text as a series of state-ments. This fruitless wondering is finally articulated by the Dean of the Cathedral, in what seems to be a sum-mary of the attitudes of 'the people'. It serves two more obvious functions as well, first by summarizing the story so far, and then in so doing by creating a pause in the action which heightens the suspense.

The word 'mervayle' is important. It seems likely that the Dean does not mean that 'It is a miracle' in a Christian sense, but rather a less specific, 'It is a wonder'. Various synonyms for 'wonder', e.g. 'ferly' have set the context for this. The bishop's first words, 'þou says soþe,' have great dramatic force, emphasizing the Dean's conclusion that they are in the presence of a 'mervayle'. It is the bishop who shifts the use of the word to the more specific sense,[45] and he goes on to include them all in it. The poet is calling both the Londoners and his audience to witness.

The judge's first utterance is followed by the poet's description of its effect:

Quil he in spelunke þus spake þer sprange in þe pepull
In al þis worlde no worde, ne wakenyd no noice,
Bot al as stille as þe ston stoden and listonde,
Wyt meche wonder forwrast, and wepid ful mony.

(11.217-20)

It cannot be argued that these lines serve merely to interrupt a long speech to solve the problem which arises in a dramatic reading when a long exposition is necessary and the author is at pains to prevent boredom. He might have made this scene simply a dialogue between priest and judge, but includes the crowd because he wants to emphasize their presence, their reactions, and the strengthening of their faith which comes from the miracle:

þen wos louyng oure Lord wyt loues vp halden,
Meche mournyng and myrthe was mellyd to geder.

45 The *OED* lists 'mervayle' as 'wonder' for this period, specifically in the phrase (s.v.5) 'It is marvel' (from Wyclif, 'It is grett meruaile þat god...distroieþ not alle þis cursed peple'). This use is found in the North West Midlands through the sixteenth century.

þai passyd forthe in procession and alle þe pepull
                                                folowid,
And all þe belles in þe burghe beryd at ones.
                                        (11.349-52)

Since 'St.Erkenwald' is not a saint's life, the poet
is concerned not so much with a particular protagonist
as with the whole situation. Neither bishop nor judge is
a 'character' in the sense in which Chaucer's Troilus is
a character, or in which we can analyze Gawain's 'char-
acter' in terms of human complexity. In his delineation
of the bishop and judge the poet is not concerned with
the quirks which individualize them, but in the parallels
and stock qualities which make them typical. The pagan
was a judge, seated in the Triapolitan Temple, who
taught the law to a difficult people; the saint, who is
travelling to oversee his flock when the poem begins, is
seated in St.Paul's ('þat was þe temple triapolitan')
where he, too, teaches the law to a people who are
troubled. I have suggested that the poet makes the judge
set up a legal case for his own salvation. The technique
is a standard one in medieval rhetoric, repetition with
variations.

Suspense is built up when the judge evades the main
issue in his long description of his life (11.225-45).
The poet summarizes the gist of the speech in a single
statement, which he then emphasizes by repeating it and
strengthening the effect of it in our minds. In fact we
are hearing a subtle plea; in a sense the judge is still
in court, and the periphrases for God consistently refer
to God's role as judge.[46] The reiterated word 'right'
appears in continually changing position. Not always the
alliterating word, it has been slipped into the lines in
a variety of ways:

And for I rewardid euer riȝt þai raght me the septre.
                                        (1.256)

46 See Benson, 1965; Clark, *MLN*, 1950.

41

Bot þe riche kyng of reson, þat riȝt euer alowes.

(1.267)

And most he menskes men for mynnyng of riȝtes. (1.269)

And if renkes for riȝt þus me arayed has,
He has lant me to last þat loues ryȝt best. (11.271-2)

The bishop asked after the judge's soul in his first ad-
dress (1.188); he hears about the judge's life, and
about legendary British history, but the judge ignores
his primary question. It is not until 1.273, almost one
hundred lines later, that the bishop reminds the judge
of his unanswered question; he puts it again, almost as
a challenge, repeating the words in the second phrase,
'sayes þou of þi saule', then 'fforþi say me of þi soule'
(11.273, 279). The assumption Erkenwald makes, and which
we share, stems from a subtle use of language: the poet
has him state his questions as an 'if...then' clause.
The general law to which he appeals is that of the Athan-
asian Creed: *Qui bona egerunt ibunt in vitam eternam,
Qui vero mala, in ignum eternum*. But the judge's soul is
in Limbo.

Let us look closely at two key passages.

Bot þe riche kyng of reson, þat riȝt euer alowes,
And loues al þe lawes lely þat longen to trouthe
And most he menskes men for mynnyng of riȝtes
þen for al þe meritorie medes þat men on molde vsen.
And if renkes for riȝte þus me arayed has,
He has lant me to last þat loues ryȝt best.

(11.267-72)

(The noble ruler of wisdom, who always sanctions right-
eous behaviour, and justly loves all the laws that
yearn after truth [has preserved me]. And he honours
men more for commemorating righteous deeds than for
all the gifts earthly men use to be deserving of re-
ward. If men have arrayed me thus for righteousness,
He, who loves righteousness best, has granted that I
should be preserved.)

42

The judge's claim that good works performed in a vaguely defined yearning after Truth are more deserving of reward than the insincere gifts with which earthly men try to bribe their way into heaven was common enough social criticism. His words resemble those of Langland, both in his social criticism and in his claim for the worthiness of following one's best perception of Truth. 'Lely', a word quite often found in conjunction with 'love' in alliterative poetry, seems here to imply that God's approbation is both just and right. 'Lely' is intensive, and appears in an emphatic position where rhythm, ornate alliteration, and the extended half-line work together. If we look at the uses of 'law' throughout the poem we see the poet playing on the ambiguities of the word. Law can mean the specific rules by which society governs its members or the philosophy which underlies society or God's free committal of his absolute power to a world of order. The judge is certainly a 'lede of the laghe' in the first sense; he must show himself a worthy member of the world of Christian Law as well.

Erkenwald appeals to the wider interpretation of law when he says that if in fact the judge was a righteous man God ought to have bestowed some measure of grace upon him, which assumes that God's law extends through all time. The judge responds with the objection that he lived in ignorance of the dispensation of Christian law and therefore fails only in the first sense, and 'fails' implies 'lack' more than an unsuccessful attempt. His cry against his fate implies his coming salvation:

Quat wan we wyt oure wele dede þat wroghtyn ay riȝt,
Quen we are dampned dulfully into þe depe lake
And exilid fro þat soper so, þat solempne fest:
þer richely hit arne refetyd þat after right hungride.
(11.301-4)

(What did we, who always behaved righteously, gain by our good works, when we are grievously damned into the deep lake and exiled from the supper, that solemn feast where those who hungered after righteousness are

43

worthily refreshed.)

The judge voices his appeal in Scriptural terms. The echo of the Beatitudes (1.304) is itself evidence of the judge's 'firm belief' — one of the two qualifications for salvation.[47] The judge insists on this metaphor, and his longing and his belief (for even in the dark of Limbo the Incarnation was revealed) move the bishop to 'lavande' tears. The word carries the event in it: 'lavande' means not only 'streaming' but 'washing', and specifically the sacred washing that cleans a man's soul.

The poet of 'St.Erkenwald' has weighed the claims of 'belief' and 'baptism'. His poem is an attempt to reconcile the two, and to make two theological opinions accord.

47 Cf. the quotation of the Beatitudes in *Patience*:

þay ar happen also þat hungeres after ryȝt,
For þay schal frely be refete ful of alle gode.
(11.19-20)

(Ed. J.J.Anderson, 1972)

44

A NOTE ON AUTHORSHIP

THE PROBLEM OF the authorship of 'St.Erkenwald' arose in the nineteenth century when scholars attributed the alliterative poems, with their remarkable similarities of phrase and technique, either to one author, e.g. Huchown, or to a school. Because 'St.Erkenwald' seemed to come in the forefront of second-best poems it was assigned to the hand of the man who had written the four poems in Cotton Nero A.x, *Gawain and the Green Knight*, *Pearl*, *Patience*, and *Purity*, though the hand was assumed to be trembling slightly with age. Starting with this assumption, it was almost inevitable that Knigge, who first analyzed the language of the five-poem group, should have declared that the linguistic anomalies in 'St. Erkenwald' were due to scribal corruption. The simpler solution to the difficulties of the different dialect of 'St.Erkenwald' would have been to say — as we now do — that we do not know who wrote the poem. Once Knigge had 'proved' the *Gawain*-poet's authorship, the obvious next step was to divide the poem into quatrains, as the 'original' must have been divided, although here again anomalies abounded.[48] The 'defective stanzas' were accounted for as another sure sign that the poet, who had been able to control the complex forms of *Gawain* and *Pearl*, was now losing his grip. The 'boredom theory' was used as well: perhaps the poet was not very interested in his story— although how that could be said of a poem as complex as 'St.Erkenwald' is hard to understand. Al-

---

48 Max Kaluza, 1892, divided the poem into eleven sections of four quatrains each— though he had to admit that three of his quatrains were simply defective, as there did not seem to be lines omitted. Mabel Day, 1931-2, rejected Kaluza's larger divisions, but accepted the quatrains. Wherever else in Harley 2250 some stanzaic organization exists it is indicated by the use of red ink, which is absent in this poem.

though the occasional reviewer demurred (e.g. O.F.Emerson in *Speculum*, 1927), the quatrain arrangement was followed by Gollancz, Savage, and most, if not all, of the translators of the poem. The theory that the author of *Sir Gawain* had written the poem was accepted by both Gollancz and Savage, as well as by Oakden in his *Alliterative Poetry*, in the face of vastly diminished evidence in the theory's favour.[49]

As our understanding of the conventions of alliterative poetry increases, the similarities between 'St. Erkenwald' and the *Gawain*-group appear less significant. Indeed, the closest poem to 'St.Erkenwald' in terms of dialect and phraseology seems to be *The Destruction of Troy*, though no one has argued for common authorship of these two poems.

All this speculation has made little difference to studies of the *Gawain*-poet; 'St.Erkenwald' has usually

49 Oakden, 1930, 1935, (especially Vol.II, pp.179-81, 267-312), attempted to show that the *Gawain*-poet had a distinctive vocabulary which became obvious when the five-poem group was compared with other alliterative poetry. He ignored the 'subject' factor: poems on religious themes are more likely to share vocabulary with each other than with poems about war. Because he set up his experiment to find the similarities between 'St.Erkenwald' and the four Cotton Nero poems, those were what he found. Had he made the same detailed comparison of 'characteristic' words with either *Morte Arthure* or *The Destruction of Troy*, he would have reached the same result. Only two words seem to be found exclusively in the five-poem group: *roynisch* and *nourne*. But these two words appear in dialectally different forms and with slightly different meanings. The 'statistical evidence' dissolves when one has examined the bias of the original questions. It should be added that Oakden was drawing evidence from Gollancz's heavily emended text, which added to the bias of his word-count.

been mentioned and then ignored. Occasionally doubts have been raised about its place in the canon, but by and large it has been accepted as a step-child which could with reason be neglected.

In 1965 L.D.Benson attempted to refute finally the theory of common authorship. His argument is worth repeating. 'St.Erkenwald' is found, he reminds us, in a different and later manuscript and in a different dialect from the Cotton Nero poems. The poem's subject matter is London not the West Midlands, though this could be due to artistic reasons. The stylistic traits which once seemed peculiar to the *Gawain*-poet now appear common to the alliterative tradition as a whole: the formulaic poetic vocabulary, shared words, the clusters of similes and the use of the absolute adjective, and periphrases for God, the similarities of alliteration and meter. To these may be added the love of set piece descriptions of clothes and furniture, and the delight in legal terminology. Moreover there are striking differences between the styles of 'St.Erkenwald' and the *Gawain*-group. The *Gawain*-poet uses a variety of 'traditional alliterative synonyms for 'man' as head words; 'St.Erkenwald' does not. The *Gawain*-poet's vocabulary is considerably richer than that of the man who wrote 'St. Erkenwald'.

To this already convincing argument may be added further that the poet of 'St.Erkenwald' has theological interests different from those of the *Gawain*-poet. The latter was concerned with purity; the former with good works and man's righteousness as a claim on God's grace. The salvation of the righteous heathen is not a 'virtue' like 'patience' or 'purity' or 'truth'. The *Gawain*-poet seems to have thought of salvation as a free gift; to the poet of 'St.Erkenwald' salvation can be merited by righteousness. Finally, though incidentally, the completely masculine London world of 'St.Erkenwald' is very unlike what we would expect from the poet who wrote the Cotton Nero works.

The 'authorship problem' is due to an historical

47

accident: what seemed a reasonable argument to the men who discovered the alliterative revival seems less so today. It is possible, though extremely unlikely, that the man who wrote the *Gawain*-poems also wrote the poem in Harley 2250. It hardly requires Occam's razor to maintain that the burden of proof must lie with those who wish to assert common authorship. Although no 'proof' either way can be conclusive, it is most sensible to assume that 'St.Erkenwald' is a single anonymous poem, which survives because someone mistook it for a saint's life or legend and so included it in a manuscript of devotional readings. We do the poem no disservice to study it on its own.[50]

50 Most recently C.J.Peterson, 1974, has attempted to prove that *Pearl* and 'St.Erkenwald' were both written by I. de Masse, who hid an anagram of his name in the alliterating or final words of certain significant lines. His procedure for choosing which lines are in this way 'significant' is to follow an ingenious and arbitrary arrangement of their numbers. There is in fact no basis for his attribution.

BIBLIOGRAPHY

1 Texts and translations of 'St.Erkenwald'.

BM Ms. Harley 2250, ff. 72^v-75^r.
I.Gollancz, *St.Erkenwald* (London, 1922).
C.Horstmann, *Altenglischen Legenden* (Heilbronn, 1881).
H.L.Savage, *St.Erkenwald* (New Haven, 1926).
John Gardner, *The Complete Works of the Gawain-Poet*
    (Chicago, 1965).
Brian Stone, *The Owl and the Nightingale, Cleanness, St.*
    Erkenwald (Harmondsworth, 1971).

2 Other alliterative works quoted.

F.J.Amours, 'The Knightly Tale of Golagros and Gawane'
    in *Scottish Alliterative Poems* (Edinburgh, 1897).
J.J.Anderson, *Patience* (Manchester, repr. 1972).
E.Brock, ed., *Morte Arthure*, EETS O.S.8 (London, 1865).
G.L.Brook and R.F.Leslie, eds., *Laʒamon's Brut*, vol.1,
    EETS O.S.250 (London, 1963).
K.D.Buelbring, ed., *Earliest English Prose Psalter*,
    EETS O.S.97 (London, 1891).
N.Davis, et al, eds., *Sir Gawain and the Green Knight*
    (Oxford, 1967).
Robert J.Gates, ed., *The Awntyrs off Arthure at the*
    Terne Wathelyne (Philadelphia, 1969).
I.Gollancz, ed., *Death and Liffe* (London, 1930).
I.Gollancz, *A Good Short Debate Between Winner and Wast-*
    er (London, 1920).
E.Kölbing and Mabel Day, eds., *The Siege of Jerusalem*,
    EETS O.S.188 (London, 1931).
Alice Miskimin, ed., *Susannah* (New Haven, 1969).
R.Morris, ed., *Cleanness* in *Early English Alliterative*
    Poems, EETS O.S.1 (London, 1867).
M.Y.Offord, ed., *The Parlement of The Thre Ages*, EETS
    O.S.246 (London, 1959).
G.A.Panton and D.Donaldson, eds., *The Gest Hystoriale of*
    the Destruction of Troy,EETS O.S.39, 56 (London, 1869,
    1874).

W.W.Skeat, ed., 'Alexander A' in *William of Palerne*,
    EETS E.S.1 (London, 1867).
W.W.Skeat, *The Alliterative Romance of Alexander and
    Dindimus*, EETS E.S.31 (London, 1878).
W.W.Skeat, *The Alliterative Romance of Joseph of Arima-
    thea, or The Holy Grail*, EETS O.S.44 (London, 1870).
W.W.Skeat, *Piers Plowman B-Text*, EETS O.S.38 (London,
    1869).
W.W.Skeat, *Piers Plowman C-Text, Richard the Redeles*,
    EETS O.S.54 (London, 1873).

3 Sources and Reference

Analecta Bollandiana (Paris and Rome, 1866–).
Sir George Armytage and J.P.Rylands, eds., *Pedigrees
    Made at the Visitation of Cheshire*, 1613... (London,
    1909).
C.M.Briquet, *Les Filigranes*, 4 vols. (Geneva, 1907).
Carleton Brown, *A Register of Middle English Religious
    and Didactic Verse* (Oxford, 1916, 1920).
J.Burke Severs, *A Manual of the Writings in Middle Eng-
    lish 1050-1500*, vol.2 (Hamden, Conn., 1970).
John Capgrave, *The Kalendre of the Newe Legende of Eng-
    land* (London, 1516).
*A Catalogue of the Harleian Manuscripts in the British
    Museum* (London, 1808).
*A Catalogue of the Lansdowne Manuscripts in the British
    Museum* (London, 1812).
B.Colgrave and R.A.B.Mynors, eds., *Bede's Ecclesiastical
    History of the English People* (Oxford, 1969).
John Coulson, *The Saints* (London, Amsterdam, 1958).
H.Delehaye, *Les légendes hagiographiques* (Brussels, 1927)
Dictionary of National Biography (London, 1885–).
Wm.Dugdale, *The History of St.Paul's Cathedral in Lon-
    don...* (London, 1658).
F.S.Ellis, *The Golden Legend or Lives of the Saints, as
    Englished by W.Caxton*, 7 vols. (London, 1900).
Th.Erbe, ed., *Mirk's Festial*, EETS E.S.96 (London, 1905).
F.A.Foster, ed., *A Stanzaic Life of Christ*, EETS O.S.166
    (London, 1926).

W.Nelson Francis, *The Book of Vices and Virtues*, EETS
O.S.217 (London, 1942).

Th.Graesse, ed., Jacobi a Voragine, *Legenda Aurea...*
(Leipzig, 1850).

G.Holmstedt, ed., *Speculum Christiani*, EETS O.S.182
(London, 1933).

Carl Horstmann, ed., *Altenglischen Legenden Neue Folge*
(Heilbronn, 1881).

Carl Horstmann, *The Early South English Legendary*, EETS
O.S.87 (London, 1887).

Carl Horstmann, *Nova Legenda Anglie: as collected by
John of Tynemouth, John Capgrave, and others, and
first printed, with New Lives, by Wynkyn de Worde a.d.
mdxvi*, 2 vols. (Oxford, 1901).

N.R.Ker, *Medieval Libraries of Great Britain*, 2nd ed.
(London, 1964).

B.Kottler and A.M.Markman, *A Concordance to Five Middle
English Poems* (Pittsburgh, 1966).

W.R.Matthews and W.M.Atkins, eds., *A History of St.Paul's
Cathedral* (London, 1957).

G.Ormerod, *The History of the County Palatine and City
of Chester*, 3 vols. (London, 1957).

Nicholas Roscarrock, *Lives of British Saints*, ULC Ms.
Add.3041.

J.P.Rylands, ed., *The Visitation of Cheshire in the Year
1580...* (London, 1882)

W.Sparrow Simpson, *Documents Illustrating the History of
St.Paul's Cathedral* (London, 1880).

C.C.J.Webb, ed., *Ioannis Saresberiensis Episcopi Carno-
tensis Policratici Sive De Nugis Curialium et Vestig-
iis Philosophorum Libri VIII*, 2 vols. (Oxford, 1909).

Wells, *A Manual of the Writings in Middle English* (New
Haven, 1916-51).

John Wilson, *The English Martyrologe...*, 3rd ed. (St.
Omer, 1672).

4 Criticism and Scholarship

L.D.Benson, 'The Authorship of St.Erkenwald', *JEGP* 64

(1925), pp.393-405.

R.W.Chambers, 'Long Will, Dante, and the Righteous Heathen', *Essays and Studies* 9 (1923), pp.50-69.

John W.Clark, 'The Gawain-Poet and the Substantial Adjective', *JEGP* 44 (1950), pp.60-6.

John W.Clark, 'Paraphrases for God in the Poems Attributed to the Gawain-poet', *MLN* 65 (1950), pp.232-6.

Mabel Day, 'Strophic Division in Middle English Alliterative Verse', *Englische Studien* 66 (1931-2), pp.245-8.

Campbell Dodgson, 'An Illustration by Holbein of the Legend of Herkinbald', *Journal of the Warburg and Courtauld Institutes* 3 (1940) pp.241-3.

T.P.Dunning, 'Langland and the Salvation of the Heathen', *Medium Aevum* 12 (1943), pp.45-54.

R.W.Frank Jr., *Piers Plowman and the Scheme of Salvation* (New Haven, Conn., 1957).

Greta Hort, *Piers Plowman and Contemporary Religious Thought* (London, n.d.).

James Root Hulbert, 'The Sources of *St.Erkenwald* and *The Trental of Gregory*', *Modern Philology* 16 (1919) pp.485-93.

James Root Hulbert, 'The "West Midlands" of the English Romances', *Modern Philology* 19 (1921) pp.1-16.

James Root Hulbert, 'A Hypothesis Concerning the Alliterative Revival', *Modern Philology* 29 (1931), pp.405-22

Max Kaluza, 'Strophische gliederung in der mittelenglischen rein alliterirenden dichtung', *Englische Studien* 16 (1892), pp.169-80.

Fr.Knigge, *Die Sprache des Dichters von Sir Gawain and the Green Knight, der sogenannten Early English Alliterative Poems und De Erkenwalde* (Marburg, 1886).

Gordon Leff, *Bradwardine and the Pelagians. A Study of De Causa Dei and its Opponents* (Cambridge, 1957).

Gordon Leff, *Gregory of Rimini* (Manchester, 1961).

G.Loomis, *White Magic* (Cambridge, 1948).

Laura Hibbard Loomis, 'Erkenbald the Belgian: A Study in Medieval Exempla of Justice', *Modern Philology* 17 (1920) pp.669-78.

52

C.A.Luttrell, 'Three North West Midlands Manuscripts', *Neophilologus* 42 (1958), pp.38-50.

T.McAlindon, 'Hagiography into Art: A Study of *St.Erkenwald*', *Studies in Philology* 67 (1970) pp.472-94.

Wm.Matthews, *Medieval Secular Literature* (Berkeley, 1965).

S.Moore, S.B.Meech, and H.Whitehall, *Middle English Dialect Characteristics and Dialect Boundaries* (Ann Arbor, 1935).

George Neilson, *Huchown of the Awle Ryale* (Glasgow, 1902).

J.P.Oakden, *Alliterative Poetry in Middle English*, 2 vols. (Manchester, 1930, 1935).

H.Oberman, *Thomas Bradwardine* (Utrecht, 1957).

H.Oberman, *The Harvest of Medieval Theology* (Grand Rapids, Michigan, 1967).

Gaston Paris, 'La légende de Trajan', *Mélanges publiés par l'école des Hautes Etudies* (Paris, 1878).

R.A.Peck, 'Number Structure in *St.Erkenwald*', *Annuale Medievale* 14 (n.d.), pp.9-21.

C.J.Peterson, '*Pearl* and *St.Erkenwald*: Some Evidence for Authorship', *Review of English Studies* 25 (1974) pp.49-53.

Vincent Petronella, '*St.Erkenwald*: Style as the Vehicle for Meaning', *JEGP* 66 (1967) pp.532-40.

G.H.Russell, 'The Salvation of the Heathen: the exploration of a theme in *Piers Plowman*', *Journal of the Warburg and Courtauld Institutes* 29 (1966), pp.101-16.

Elizabeth Salter, 'The Alliterative Revival', *Modern Philology* 64 (1966-7), pp.146-50, 233-7.

Margaret Schlauch, *Medieval Literature and Its Social Foundations* (London, 1956).

M.S.Serjeantson, 'The Dialect of *St.Erkenwald*', *Review of English Studies* 3 (1927) pp.54-67, 186-203, 319-331.

A.C.Spearing, *The Gawain-Poet* (London, 1970).

J.Szövérffy, 'Heroic Tales, Medieval Legends and an Irish Story', *Zeitschrift für Celtische Philologie* 25 (1956), pp.183-210.

Th.Wolpers, *Die Englische Heiligenlegende des Mittelalters* (Tübingen, 1964).

53

ST ERKENWALD

At London in Englond no3t full long sythen, f73v
Sythen Crist suffrid on crosse & Cristendome stablyd,
Ther was a byschop in þat burghe, blessyd and sacryd:
Saynt Erkenwolde, as I hope, þat holy mon hatte.
In his tyme in þat toun þe temple alder-grattyst   5
Was drawen doun þat one dole to dedifie new
ffor hit hethen had bene in Hengyst dawes
þat þe Saxones vnsa3t haden sende hyder;
þai bete oute þe Bretons & bro3t hom into Wales
& peruertyd all þe pepul þat in þat place dwellid.   10
þen wos this reame renaide mony ronke 3eres
Til Saynt Austyn into Sandewiche was send fro þe pope.
þen prechyd he here þe pure faythe & plantyd þe trouthe
& conuertyd all þe communnates to Cristendame newe.
He turnyd temples þat tyme þat temyd to þe deuell   15
& clansyd hom in Cristes nome & kyrkes hom callid;
He hurlyd owt hor ydols & hade hym in sayntes
& chaungit cheuely hor nomes & chargit hom better.
þat ere was of Appolyn is now of Saynt Petre,
Mahon to Saynt Margrete oþer to Maudelayne,   20
þe Synagoge of þe Sonne was sett to Oure Lady,
Iubiter and Iono to Iesu oþir to Iames.
So he hom dedifiet & dyght all to dere halowes
þat ere wos sett of Sathanas in Saxones tyme.
Now þat London is neuenyd hatte þe New Troie: 25
þe metropol & þe mayster toun hit euermore has bene.
þe mecul mynster þerinne a maghty deuel aght,
& þe title of þe temple bitan was his name,
ffor he was dryghtyn derrest of ydols praysid
And þe solempnest of his sacrifices in Saxon londes.   30
þe thrid temple hit wos tolde of triapolitanes
By all Bretaynes bonkes were bot othir twayne.
Now of þis Augustynes art is Erkenwolde bischop
At loue London toun & the laghe teches,
Syttes semely in þe sege of Saynt Paule mynster   35
þat was þe temple triapolitan (as I tolde are).
þen was hit abatyd & beten doun and buggyd efte new,

A noble note for þe nones & New Werke hit hatte,
Mony a mery mason was made þer to wyrke,
40 Harde stones for to hewe wyt eggit toles;
Mony grubber in grete þe grounde for to seche
þat þe fundement on fyrst shuld þe fote halde.
& as þai makkyd & mynyd a meruayle þai founden
As ȝet in .crafty cronecles is kydde þe memorie:
45 ffor as þai dyȝt & dalfe so depe into þe erthe
þai founden fourmyt on a flore a ferly faire toumbe.
Hit was a throghe of thykke ston thryuandly hewen
Wyt gargeles garnysht aboute alle of gray marbre;
Thre sperl of þe spelunke þat spradde hit o lofte
50 Was metely made of þe marbre & menskefully planed,
& þe bordure enbelicit wyt bryȝt golde lettres.
Bot roynyshe were þe resones þat þer on row stoden;
fful verray were þe vigures— þer auisyd hom mony—
Bot all muset hit to mouthe & quat hit mene shuld.
f74r Mony clerke in þat clos with crownes ful brode
56 þer besiet hom aboute noȝt to brynge hom in wordes.
Quen tithynges token to þe toun of þe toumbe wonder
Mony hundrid hende men highid þider sone:
Burgeys boghit þerto, bedels and othir,
60 & mony a mesters mon of maners dyuerse;
Laddes laften hor werke & lepen þiderwardes,
Ronnen radly in route wyt ryngand noyce:
þer commen þider of all kynnes so kenely mony
þat as all þe worlde were þider walon wytin a honde quile.
65 Quen þe maire with his meynye þat meruaile aspied,
By assent of þe sextene þe sayntuare þai kepten,
Bede vnlouke þe lidde & lay hit byside:
þai wold loke on þat lome quat lengyd wytinne.
Wyȝt werke men wyt þat wenten þer-till,
70 Putten prises þerto, pinchid one vnder,
Kaghten by þe corners wyt crowes of yrne,
And were þe lydde neuer so large þai laide hit by sone.
Bot þen wos wonder to wale on wehes þat stoden,

55 Running title de Erkenwaldo

That myȝt not come to knowe a quontyse strange:
So was þe glode wytin gay, al wyt golde payntyd,   75
& a blisfull body opon þe bothum lyggid,
Araide on a riche wise in riall wedes,
Al wyt glisnand golde his gowne was hemmyd
Wyt mony a precious perle picchit þeron
& a gurdill of golde bigripid his mydell,   80
A meche mantel on lofte with menyuer furrit,
þe clothe of camelyn ful clene with cumly bordures,
& on his coyfe wos kest a coron ful riche
& a semely septure sett in his honde.
Als wemles were his wedes wyt-outen any tecche   85
Oþir of moulyng oþir of motes oþir moght-freten.
& als bryȝt of hor blee in blysnande hewes
As þai hade ȝepely in þat ȝorde bene ȝistur-day shapen.
& als freshe hyn þe face & the fflesh nakyd
Bi his eres & bi his hondes þat openly shewid,   90
Wyt ronke rode as þe rose & two rede lippes
As he in sounde sodanly were slippid opon slepe.
þer was spedeles space to spyr vschon oþir
Quat body hit myȝt be þat buried was ther.
'How long had he þer layne, his lere so vnchaungit,   95
& al his wede unwemmyd,' þus ylka weghe askyd.
'Hit myȝt not be bot suche a mon in my[n]de stode long.'
'He has ben kyng of þis kith as couthely hit semes.'
'He lyes doluen þus depe.' 'Hit is a derfe wonder.'
Bot summe segge couthe say þat he hym sene hade: 100
Bot þat ilke note wos noght, for nourne none couthe,
Noþir by title ne token ne by tale noþir
þat euer wos breuyt in burghe ne in boke notyd
þat euer mynnyd such a mon, more ne lasse.
þe bodeword to þe byschop was broght on a quile   105
Of þat buried body al þe bolde wonder.

74 to to knowe
94 Quat body hᵗ..hade..myȝt be (sic)
96 wegge
97 myde

þe primate wyt his prelacie was partyd fro home:
In Esex was Ser Erkenwolde an abbay to visite.
Tulkes tolden hym þe tale, wyt troubull in þe pepul,
110 And suche a cry aboute a cors crakit euer more.
f74v The bischop sende hit to blynne by bedels & lettres
And buskyd þiderwarde by tyme on his blonke after.
By þat he come to þe kyrke kydde of Saynt Paule
Mony hym metten on þat meere þe meruayle to tell.
115 He passyd into his palais & pes he comaundit,
& devoydit fro þe dede & ditte þe durre after.
þe derke nyʒt ouer drofe & day belle ronge
And Ser Erkenwolde was vp in þe vghten ere þen,
þat welneghe al þe nyʒt hade nattyd his houres
120 To biseche his souerayn of his swete grace,
To vouche safe to revele hym hit by a vison or elles.
'þaghe I be vnworthi,' al wepand he sayde
Thurghe his deere debonerte, 'digne hit, my lorde,
In confirmyng þi Cristen faith fulsen me to kenne
125 þe mysterie of þis meruaile þat men opon wondres.'
& so long he grette after grace þat he graunte hade
An ansuare of þe Holy Goste, & afterwarde hit dawid,
Mynster dores were makyd opon quen matens were songen.
þe byschop hym shope solemply to synge þe heghe masse:
130 þe prelate in pontificals was prestly atyrid.
Manerly wyt his ministres þe masse he begynnes
Of Spiritus Domini for his spede on sutile wise
Wyt queme questis of þe quere, wyt ful quaynt notes.
Mony a gay grete lorde was gedrid to herken hit
135 As þe rekenest of þe reame repairen þider ofte.
Till cessyd was þe seruice & sayde þe later ende.
þen heldyt fro þe autere all þe heghe gynge.
þe prelate passid on þe playn— þer plied to hym lordes—
As riche reuestid as he was he rayked to þe toumbe.
140 Men vnclosid hym þe cloyster wyt clustred keies,
Bot pyne wos wyt þe grete prece þat passyd hym after.
þe byschop come to þe burynes, him barones besyde:

111 Running title De Sancto Erkenwaldo

58

þe maire wyt mony maȝti men & macers before hym.
þe dene of þe dere place deuisyt al on fyrst:
þe fyndynge of þat ferly. Wyt fynger he mynte,   145
'Lo, lordes,' quoth þat lede, 'suche a lyche her is
las layn loken here on logh how longe is vnknawen,
& ȝet his colour & his clothe has caȝt no defaute
Ne his lire ne þe lome þat he is layde inne.
þer is no lede opon lyfe of so long age   150
þat may mene in his mynde þat suche a mon regnyd,
Ne noþir his nome ne his note nourne of one speche.
Queþer mony porer in þis place is putte into graue
þat merkid is in oure martilage his mynde for euer.
& we haue oure librarie laited þes long seuen dayes   155
Bot one cronicle of þis kyng con we neuer fynde.
He has non layne here so long, to loke hit by kynde,
To malte so out of memorie bot meruayle hit were.'
'þou says soþe,' quoth þe segge þat sacrid was byschop,
'Hit is meruaile to men þat mountes to litell   160
Toward þe prouidens of þe prince þat paradis weldes
Quen hym luste to vnlouke þe leste of his myȝtes.
Bot quen matyd is monnes myȝt & his mynde passyd
And al his resons are to-rent & redeles he stondes,
þen lettes hit Hym ful litell to louse wyt a fynger   165
þat all þe hondes vnder heuen halde myȝt neuer.
þere as creatures crafte of counsell oute swarues
þe comforthe of þe creatore byhoues þe cure take.   f75₂
& so do we now oure dede, deuyne we no fyrre.
To seche þe sothe at oure selfe ȝee se þer no bote.   170
Bot glow we all opon Godde & His grace aske,
þat careless is of counsell & comforthe to sende,
& þat in fastynge of ȝour faith & of fyne bileue
I shal auay ȝow so verrayly of vertues His
þat ȝe may leue vpon long þat he is Lord myȝty   175
& fayne ȝour talent to fulfille if ȝe hym frende leues.'

146 lyche God^her is (sic)
155 latted
168 Running title De Stō Erkenwaldo

59

Then he turnes to þe toumbe & talkes to þe corce;
Lyftand vp his egh lyddes he loused such wordes:
'Now, lykhame þat þ[us] lies, layne þou no lenger.
180 Sythen Iesu has iuggit today his ioy to be schewyd
Be þou bone to his bode, I bydde in his behalue:
As he was bende on a beme quen he his blode schedde,
As þou hit wost wyterly & we hit wele leuen,
Ansuare here to my sawe, councele no trouthe.
185 Sithen we wot not qwo þou art, witere vs þi seluen
In worlde quat weghe þou was & quy þou þus ligges.
How long þou has layne here & quat lagh þou vsyt,
Queþer art þou ioyned to ioy oþer iuggid to pyne.'
Quen þe segge hade þus sayde & syked þerafter
190 þe bryȝt body in þe burynes brayed a litell,
& wyt a drery dreme he dryues owte wordes
þurghe sum lant goste lyf of hym þat al redes.
'Bisshop,' quoth þis ilke body, 'þi boode is me dere.
I may not bot boghe to þi bone for bothe myn eghen.
195 To þe name þat þou neuenyd has & nournet me after
Al heuen and helle heldes to, & erthe bitwene.
ffirst to say the þe sothe quo my selfe were:
One þe vnhapnest hathel þat euer on erth ȝode.
Neuer kyng ne caysere ne ȝet no knyȝt nothyre,
200 Bot a lede of þe laghe þat þen þis londe vsit.
I was committid & made a mayster mon here,
To sit upon sayd causes þis cite I ȝemyd
Vnder a prince of parage of paynymes laghe
(& vche segge þat him sewid þe same fayth trowid).
205 þe lengthe of my lying here, þat is a lewid date,
Hit [is] to mec[h]e to any mon to make of a nommbre.
After þat Brutus þis burghe had buggid on fyrste
Noȝt bot fife hundred ȝere þer aghtene wontyd
Before þat kynned ȝour Criste by Cristen acounte—
210 A þousande ȝere & þritty mo & ȝot threnen aght.
I was an heire of anoye in þe New Troie

177 Two-line red capital T
179 þu

60

In þe regne of þe riche kyng þat rewlit vs þen,
The bolde Breton, Ser Belyn, — Ser Berynge was his brothir.
Mony one was þe busmare boden hom bitwene
ffor hor wrakeful werre quil hor wrath lastyd.   215
þen was I iuge here enioynyd in gentil lawe.'
Quil he in spelunke þus spake þer sprange in þe pepull
In al þis world no worde, ne wakenyd no noice,
Bot al as stille as þe ston stoden & listonde,
Wyt meche wonder forwrast & wepid ful mony.   220
The bisshop biddes þat body, 'Biknowe þe cause,
Sithen þou was kidde for no kynge, quy þou þe croun weres?
Quy haldes þou so heghe in honde þe Septre
& hades no londe of lege men ne life ne lym aghtes?'
'Dere Ser,' quoth the dede Body, 'Deuyse þe, I thenke.   f75v
Al was hit neuer my wille þat wroght þus hit were.   226
I wos deputate & domesmon vnder a duke noble
& in my power þis place was putte al-to-geder.
I iustifiet þis ioly toun on gentil wise
& euer in fourme of gode faithe, more þen fourty wynter   230
þe folke was felonse & fals & frowarde to reule.
I hent harmes ful ofte to holde hom to riȝt.
Bot for wothe ne wele ne wrathe ne drede
Ne for maystrie ne for mede ne for no monnes aghe
I remewit neuer fro þe riȝt by reson myn awen.   235
ffor to dresse a wrang dome no day of my lyue
Declynet neuer my consciens for couetise on erthe
In no gynful iugement no iapes to make.
Were a renke neuer so riche, for reuerens sake,
Ne for no monnes manas, ne meschefe, ne routhe,   240
Non gete me fro þe heghe gate to glent out of ryȝt.
Als ferforthe as my faith confourmyd my hert.
þaghe had bene my fader bone I bede hym no wranges,
Ne fals fauour to my fader þaghe fell hym be hongyt.
& for I was ryȝtwys & reken & redy of þe laghe,   245
Quen I deghed for dul denyed all Troye,
Alle menyd my dethe, þe more & the lasse,

225 Running title De Stō Erkenwaldo

61

& þus to bounty my body þai buriet in golde,
Cladden me for þe curtest þat courte couthe þen holde,
250 In mantel for þe mekest & monlokest on benche,
Gurden me for þe gouernour & graythist of Troie,
ffurrid me for þe fynest of faith me wytinne;
ffor þe honour of myn honeste of heghest enprise
þai coronyd me þe kidde kynge of kene iustises,
255 þer euer wos tronyd in Troye oþir trowid euer shulde
And for I rewardid euer riȝt þai raght me the septre.'
þe bisshop baythes hym ȝet wyt bale at his hert
þaghe men menskid him so, how hit myȝt worthe
þat his clothes were so clene, 'In cloutes, me thynkes,
260 Hom burde haue rotid & bene rent in rattes longe sythen.'
þi body may be enbawmyd, hit bashis me noght
þat hit thar ryue ne route ne no ronke wormes.
Bot þi coloure ne þi clothe I know in no wise
How hit myȝt lye by monnes lore & last so longe.'
265 'Nay, bisshop,' quoth þat body, 'embawmyd wos I neuer,
Ne no monnes counsell my cloth has kepyd vnwemmyd,
Bot þe riche kyng of reson, þat riȝt euer alowes,
& loues al þe lawes lely þat longen to trouthe;
& moste he menskes men for mynnyng of riȝtes
270 þen for al þe meritorie medes þat men on molde vsen.
& if renkes for riȝt þus me arayed has,
He has lant me to last þat loues ryȝt best.'
'Ȝea, bot sayes þou of þi saule,' þen sayd þe bisshop.
'Quere is ho stablid & stadde if þou so streȝt wroghtes.
275 He þat rewardes vche a renke as he has riȝt seruyd
Myȝt euel forgo the to gyfe of his grace summe brawnche.
ffor as he says in his sothe psalmyde writtes,
"þe skilfulle & þe vnskathely skelton ay to me."
fforþi say me of þi soule, in sele quere ho wonnes,
280 And of the rich restorment þat raȝt hyr Oure Lorde.'
þen hummyd he þat þer lay & his hedde waggyd,
& gefe a gronying ful grete & to Godde sayde,
'Maȝty maker of men, thi myghtes are grete.
How myȝt þi mercy to me amounte any tyme?

Nas I a paynym vnpreste þat neuer thi plite knewe,
Ne þi mesure of þi mercy ne þi mecul vertue, 286
Bot ay a freke faitheles þat faylid þi laghes
þat euer þou, Lord, wos louyd in? Allas, þe harde stoundes!
I was non of þe nommbre þat þou wyt noy boghtes
Wyt þe blode of thi body upon þe blo rode. 290
Quen þou herghedes Helle hole & hentes hom þeroute
þi loffynge oute of Limbo þou laftes me þer!
& þer sittes my soule, þat se may no fyrre,
Dwynande in þe derke deth þat dyȝt vs oure fader,
Adam, oure alder, þat ete of þat appull 295
þat mony a plyȝtles pepul has poysned for euer.
Ȝe were entouchid wyt his tethe & take in þe glotte,
Bot mendyd wyt a medecyn ȝe are made forto lyuye
þat is fulloght in fonte wyt faitheful bileue.
& þat han we myste alle merciles, myself & my soule. 300
Quat wan we wyt oure wele dede þat wroghtyn ay riȝt,
Quen we are dampnyd dulfully into þe depe lake
& exilid fro þat soper so, þat solempne fest:
þer richely hit arne refetyd þat after right hungride.
My soule may sitte þer in sorow & sike ful colde 305
Dymly in þat derke dethe— þer dawes neuer morowen,
Hungrie in wyt Helle hole & herken after meeles,
Longe er ho þat soper se oþir segge hyr to lathe.'
þus dulfully þis dede body deuisyt hit sorowe
þat alle wepyd for woo þe wordes þat herden. 310
& the bysshop balefully bere doun his eghen
þat hade no space to speke, so spakly he ȝoskyd
Til he toke hym a tome & to þe toumbe lokyd,
To þe liche þer hit lay, wyt lauande teres.
'Oure lord lene,' quoth þat lede, 'þat þou lyfe hades 315
By Goddis leue as longe as I myȝt lacche water
& cast vpon þi fair cors & carpe þes wordes,
'I folwe þe in þe Fader nome & his fre Childes
& of þe gracious Holy Goste" & not one grue lenger,

285 Running title De Stō Erkenwaldo
306 Dynly

63

320 þen þof þou droppyd doun dede hit daungerde me lasse.'
Wyt þat worde þat he warpyd þe wete of eghen
& teres trillyd adoun & on þe toumbe lighten,
& one felle on his face & þe freke syked.
þen sayd he wyt a sadde soun, 'Oure Sauyoure be louyd!
325 How herid be þou, heghe God & þi hende modir,
& blissid be þat blisful houre þat ho the bere in,
& also be þou, Bysshop, þe bote of my sorowe,
& the relefe of þe lodely lures þat my soule has lenyd in!
ffor þe wordes þat þou werpe & þe water þat þou sheddes—
330 þe bryзt bourne of þin eghen— my bapteme is worthyn!
þe fyrst slent þat on me slode slekkyd al my tene.
Ryзt now to soper my soule is sette at þe table.
ffor wyt þe wordes & þe water þat weshe vs of payne
Liзtly lasshit þer a leme loghe in þe abyme
335 þat spakly sprent my spyrit wyt vnsparid murthe
Into þe cenacle solemply þer soupen all trew,
& þer a marciall hyr mette wyt menske aldergrattest
& wyt reuerence a rowme he raзt hyr for euer.
I heere þerof my heghe God & also þe, Bysshop,
340 ffro bale has broзt vs to blis— blessid þou worth.'
f77v Wyt þis cessyd his sowne, sayd he no more,
Bot sodenly his swete chere swyndid & faylid,
And alle þe blee of his body wos blakke as þe moldes,
As roten as þe rottok þat rises in powder.
345 ffor assone as þe soule was sesyd in blisse
Corrupt was þat oþir crafte þat couert þe bones.
ffor the ay-lastande life þat lethe shall neuer
Deuoydes vche a vayne glorie þat vayles so litelle.
þen wos louyng oure Lord wyt loues vp halden.,
350 Meche mournyng & myrthe was mellyd togeder.
þai passyd forthe in procession & alle þe pepull folowid
And all þe belles in þe burghe beryd at ones.

341 Running title De Stō Erkenwaldo ēpō

64

NOTES

1-2 'At London in England not a very long time ago, after Christ had suffered on the cross and established Christendom...' The historical opening is common in alliterative poetry. Cf. the opening of *Gawain*; *Winner and Waster*: Sythen that Bretayne was biggede, and Bruyttus it aughte. Thurgh the takynge of Troye with tresone with-inn (11.1-2). The Vita in Cotton Claudius A.V begins, 'Post passionem et resurrectionem dominicam, cum Catholica fides per orbem terrarum diffusa esset...'

5 Temple alder-grattyst The poet assumes that pagan London was like Christian London: the temple which stood on the site of St Paul's was pre-eminent among pagan places of worship as St Paul's was to be among Christian ones.

7 Hengyst Vortigern, ruler of the Britons, invited the Saxon Hengist to settle in Kent, with the understanding that Hengist and his men would keep other Saxon invaders out of Britain. Once, however, Hengist's men were well established, they turned on Vortigern and invited other Saxon tribes to join them. The Britons managed to hold the Saxons at bay for some time but eventually they were driven back into, among other places, Wales. This history was widely available in the works of Bede, Geoffrey of Monmouth, and Geoffrey's translators, Robert Wace and Laʒamon.

12 Saynt Austyn into Sandewiche. According to Bede (*Eccl. Hist.* I.25) Pope Gregory sent Augustine and his companions to convert the British from the Pelagian heresy and to convince them to submit to the authority of Rome. After certain delays they landed, and first preached, at the Isle of Thanet (Kent). Sandwich was, in the poet's time, a logical place to have them arrive at; it is the port from which men depart for the continent throughout *Morte Arthure*, e.g. 11.447, 635.

15-24   The poet's list of pagan gods is a combination
of imagination and alliterative commonplaces. Appolyn,
perhaps originally a French form, is found throughout
alliterative poetry, e.g. *Alex B* 1.701, *Joseph of
Arimathie*, 11.376, 380. Iubiter is likewise common.
Mahoun means 'devil', from the confused belief that it
was the Prophet and not Allah who was worshipped. Bede
(*Eccl. Hist.*I, 33) and the Vita in Cot. Claud. A.V tell
us that Augustine restored a Christian Church from the
period of Roman Britain and that he founded the church
of Sts.Peter and Paul at Canterbury.

25 New Troie   When Brutus, the eponymous founder of
Britain, established his city he called it after the
city of his ancestors. In Laʒamon's *Brut* Diana appears
to him in a dream to tell him what land he and his
people are to settle (Cf. Aeneid III, 159-171), 'ane
neowe Troye þar makian' (Caligula, 1.625). Brutus finds
a pleasant spot on the banks of the Thames 'þa Brutus
hefde imaked þa hehge burh. þa Neowe Troie was ihaten'
(1.1037).

27 Maghty Devel   The poet continues his specious hist-
orical setting: the devil has no name because the poet
does not know it.

29 Dryghtyn   A common synonym for God, cf. *Parl.3.Ages*
'There dere Drighyyne this daye dele vs of thi blysse'
(1.664).

30 Solempnest of his sacrifices   Cf. *Alex B* 'Wiþ solem-
pne sacrifice · serue hem at ones' (1.735).

31 Triapolitanes   The poet is again making the past
like the present. London, York, and Canterbury were the
three most important ecclesiastical centres in the Eng-
land of his day. Perhaps he has made up this Greek-
sounding word to suggest a similar pagan hierarchy (from
tria + polites). The occurrence of 'communates' suggests
that he may have used some glossary— but neither word is
to be found in any printed glossary.

37 Abatyd and beten doun   Cf. *Siege of Jerusalem*
'Noþer tymbr ne tre · temple ne oþer / Bot doun beten &
brent · into blake erþe (11.1287-8); Mandeville's
Travels, 'Jerusalem hathe often tyme ben destroyed, and
the walles abated and beten doun and tombled in to the
Vale' (p.95).

38 New Werke   This section of St. Paul's belonged to
the thirteenth century, not to the seventh.

39-41   Cf. *Siege of Jerusalem* 'With mynours & masouns.
myn þey bygonne/ Grobben fast in þe grounde...' (11.
1107-8), 'Hewen þrow hard ston · hadde hem to grounde'
(1.1279).

41-2   'Many diggers excavated the ground to be sure
that the primary foundations would hold the bases of the
columns'.

46 Ferly faire toumbe   Cf. *Joseph of A.* 'And a ferly
feir mon · and witerli him rewes' (1.154).

52 Roynyshe   An unusual word, found as 'runish' in the
works of the *Gawain*-poet and usually translated as
'rough'. But here the sense seems to be that although
the letters cut into the tomb were legible, no one could
decipher the inscription.

59-64   The society the poet describes is all male.

60 Mesters mon   Master's man ought to mean apprentice,
but the contrast in 1.61 suggests that it might be
'Mester-mon', i.e. skilled craftsman, chief or leader,
that the poet originally wrote. Cf. *Dest. Troy* 1.1592.

64 Honde quile   A common filler, cf. *P3 Ages* 'And ʒe
will, ledys, me listen ane hande-while (1.406); *S.J.* 'Bot
alle hapneþ to hele · in one hand whyle (1.168); *Dest.
Troy* 'Haile from the heuyn in a hond while' and 'Her-
kinvs now a hondewile of a hegh cas' (11.406, 7346).

73-4   An example of compressed syntax: 'But then there
was a wonder to think about for the men that stood there,

who were not able to understand this strange thing.'

75-92   The poet has reversed the usual order, from head to toe, of the topos of description of a person. Cf. the description of Ʒouthe in *P3 Ages* ll.109-135; Sir Galarone in *Awntyrs of Ar.* XXX-XXXI.

77   The judge is dressed both like a king (crown and sceptre) and like a judge (coif and miniver trim). Cf. *Richard the Redeles* III, 320 'þey cared ffor no coyffes · þat men of court vsyn.'

79 Precious perle   Cf. *S.J.* 'With many preciose perle & pured stones' (1.472).

80 And a gurdill of golde bigripid his mydell   Cf. *Winner and Waster* 'Full gayly was that grete lorde girde in the myddis' (1.95); *S.J.* 'No gretter þan a grehounde · to grype on þ medil' (1.1248).

84 And a semely septure sett in his honde   Cf. *Death and Liffe* 'With a scepter sett in her hand of selcoth gemmes' (1.96).

87 Bryʒt of hor blee   Cf. *Death and Liffe* 'Shee was brighter of her blee then was the bright sonn' (1.6).

88 Ʒepely in þat ʒorde   'As if they had just been made there'.

98 Kyng of þis kith   Cf. *Winner and Waster* 'Now the kyng of this kythe, kepe hym our Lorde' (1.69); *P. 3 Ages* 'And was kyng of kith & þe Crown hadde' (1.466).

99 Dolven þus depe   Cf. *Morte Arthure* 'depe dolven and dede, dyked in moldez' (1.975).

101 Nourne (also ll.152, 195)   A word that apparently occurs only in this poem and those of the *Gawain*-poet. See glossary.

108 Esex   Another indication that the poet had read a Vita of St. Erkenwald. The nunnery which Erkenwald founded for his sister was at Barking, Essex.

110   Compressed syntax: 'that' understood. 'And that such a cry about a corpse continually increased.'

117 Þe derke nyȝt over drofe   Cf. *Dest. Troy* 'When the day ouer drogh · & the derk entred (1.7348).

121 Vison   Perhaps corresponds with *visio*, a true prophetic dream, in medieval dream theory. The terms are, however, unstable, as Chaucer notes, *The House of Fame*, 1-12; and cf. W.C.Curry, *Chaucer and the Medieval Sciences*, 1926, repr. 1960, 195-240.

123 Debonerté   Usually used in a courtly context, but also to be found in a translation of Psalm 64 (65), verse 12 'þou shalt blesce to þe time of þe ȝere of þe de-bonairte; and þy feldes shul be fulfild of plente', *The Earliest English Prose Psalter*.

126 Grette after grace   Cf. *Alex. B.* 'Miche gretiþing of grace · & grauntinge of ioie' and 'When ȝe hem greden of griþ to graunte ȝour bone' (11.254, 764).

132 Spiritus Domini   In the *Sarum Missal*, the Missal used in England during the fourteenth and fifteenth centuries, these are the opening (and thus identifying) words of the Votive Mass of the Holy Spirit (see J.Wickham Legg, ed. *The Sarum Missal*, Oxford, 1916, p.385). Votive masses are chosen by the celebrant in special circumstances. This mass emphasizes prayers to the Holy Spirit for grace; it uses two lessons which, particularly in the context of the poem, indicated a reliance on the efficacy of the Holy Spirit (see Introd.) The second lesson is taken from John XIV 23-31. It is here that we find the promise which must have moved the poet: Respondit Jesus, et dixit ei: Si quis diligit me, sermonem meum servabit, et Pater meus diliget eum, et ad eum veniemus, et mansionem apud eum faciemus. 'Jesus answered and said unto him, If a man love me, he will keep my words: and my Father will love him, and we will come unto him and make our abode with him.'

134 Mony a gay grete lorde   See note to line 80.

138 Pontificals   Erkenwald, still dressed for the mass, is 'girded' for his task.

142 Him barons beside   A common construction in alliterative poetry. 'His barons beside him.'

148 Defaute   The physical spotlessness of the corpse and its coverings suggests that it is spiritually *immaculate* as well.

160-61   'That which is a miracle to man amounts to a little thing for the providence of God (þe prince þat paradis weldes) when He chooses to unleash the least part of his strength.' Cf. *Winner and Waster* 'It es plesynge to the Prynce þat paradise wroghte' (1.296).

167-8   Repeats the contrast of ll. 160-1 with compressed syntax. 'When man's ability has failed it behoves him to take comfort in the power of the Creator.'

177   In the manuscript a break is marked here: the line begins with a small red initial letter.

180 Ioye   Not simply chosen for the alliteration. Joy is a metaphor for the grace of God in the gift of salvation. Cf. *Piers Plowman* B XIX.62, C XXII.66.

181-98   Gawain similarly conjures an unknown 'goost' to speak in *The Awntyrs of Arthur*:

> þene coniured þe kniȝte, one Crist cone he calle:
> 'As þou was crucifiged one croys to clanse vs of syne,
> That þou sei me þe sothe wheþer þou shalle,
> And whi þou walkest þes wayes þe wodes with-in?'
> 'I was of figure and face fairest of alle...'
>   (XI 11.134-7)

Cf. also *Death and Liffe* 'Hee was bowne at his bidding, & brode on his waye' (1.216).

183-5   Cf. *Winner and Waster* 'þis wate þou full wele witterly þi-seluen.' (1.389).

70

195 To þe name þat þou nevenyd has   Cf. *P3 Ages* 'And I
schall neuen ʒow the names of nyne of the best.'

199 Never kyng ne caysere ne ʒet no knyʒt nothyre   An
alliterative formula found in Old English verse as 'cyn-
ingas...caseras'. Cf. *Winner and Waster* 'Ne es nothir
kaysser, ne kynge, ne knyghte þat the folowes (1.327);
P3 Ages 'Bothe with kynges and knyghtes and kaysers ther-
inn' (Thornton text, 1.605). *Piers Plowman* B XX.100
'Kynges and knyʒtes · Kayseres and popes.'

205 Date   As the numbers read in the manuscript they
make no sense; perhaps the poet never intended that they
should. If, however, we replace five hundred with four
hundred we get a date very close to Bede's account of
Erkenwald's consecration. The judge lived in 382 B.C.
and that was 1054 years ago. Geoffrey of Monmouth gives
no date for the rule of Belinus (1.213) but the emended
date would agree with the statement that he ruled after
the foundation of Rome by Romulus and Remus.
   This is not an unusual way of presenting a date;
Andrew of Wyntoun writes in his chronicle (completed
1420):

   A thousand a hundreth and four score
   And two yeris fully gane our
   Before Christis incarnatioun
   Off Troy was þe distructioun (11.1563-6)

Gollancz, followed by Savage, suggested a series of
emendations which satisfy a more complex calculation.
See Savage, 1926, pp.41-2.

207 Brutus   Throughout the Middle Ages, and in some
cases as late as the seventeenth century, it was believ-
ed that the Western European nations had been founded by
Trojans who fled after the sack of their city. The
French claimed Francus as their eponymous founder; the
inhabitants of Britain claimed Brutus, the descendent of
Aeneas. Geoffrey, and following him Wace and Laʒamon,
all open with his story:

þis londe was ihaten Albion · þa Brutus cum her-on.
þa nolde Brutus na-mare · þat hit swa ihaten weore.
ah scupte him nome · aefter him-seluan.
He was ihaten Brutus · þis lond he clepede Brutaine.
   (*Brut*, 11.975-8. Laȝamon's treatment is 11.36-1057).

211 An heire of anoye   Previous editors have emended
this line to make the pagan an itinerant judge. The
judge is more likely calling himself a 'child of wrath'.
Cf. *Earliest Engl. Prose Psalter* 60 (61):2, 'Ich cried
to þe fram þe cuntres of þerthe, þerwhiles þat myn hert
was anoied; þou heȝedest me in stablenes.'

213 Belyn, Berynge   Their story is told at some length
by Geoffrey of Monmouth, who calls them Belinus and
Brennius. Laȝamon (11.2141-3035), calls them Belin and
Brenne(s); his account of their 'bismares' (1.2197) is
one of the longer episodes of his history. The brothers
appear an unspecified number of years after the founda-
tion of Rome by Romulus and Remus and the prophetic
mission of Isaiah. They were famous for having conquered
Rome; Arthur uses their conquest to claim the imperial
throne for himself in *Morte Arthure* (1.277), where they
are called Belyne and Bremyne.

216 Iustifiet   Cf. the role of Christ 'and so dide
Iesus the Iewes · he Iustified and tauȝte hem / The law
of lyf · that last shall euere.' *PP* B XIX 44-5.

216 Gentil   May mean either 'pagan' (as St. Paul was
apostle to the gentiles— misunderstood in the Middle
Ages) or 'gentle', i.e. noble. Cf. *PP* B XI 240. 'Ihesu
cryste on a iewes douȝter alyzte · gentil woman þough
she were.'

217 Spelunke   In medieval Latin the classical 'speluncc-
us', cave, acquired the meaning tomb.

230 Forty   A favourite number to express 'a long time'
or 'a generation'. From Biblical usage, e.g. Moses and
the Israelites wandered in the desert forty years.

232 *Harmes*   A legal association may be implied; 'harm' could correspond to modern 'damages'.

267   Subject with verb understood to be a repetition of the verb of a previous clause. In parallel phrases the second phrase often has something left out which is to be applied from the construction of the first. Common into the late fifteenth century.

Allowes   Another word with a legal implication: a suggestion of some kind of binding agreement (see Introd.) Cf. *Alex B* 'ʒif þou our lif wole alowe · & oure lawe vse' (1.508).

268   Cf. *Winner and Waster* 'Then will scho loue hym lelely as his lyfe one.' (1.429). 'þat loued ʒou full lelly' *R. the Redeles* 1.57, 'And whan I loue lelly · our lorde and alle other'. *PP* B XV 33.

269   Cf. *Alex B* '& he is mensked þe mor · amongus ʒou alle' (1.1040).

272   Cf. *Joseph of A.* "Now I þonke my lord", seide Ioseph, "þat lente me of his grace" (1.5).

278 Psalm   I have been unable to find an exact source for this in the psalms, though Psalm 23, 4 is close. Gollancz suggested that the poet was translating Psalm 14. Possibly a formula. Cf. *R. the Redeles* II. 105 'Or ellis for a skylle · þat skathed ʒoure-self.'

283 *Maʒty maker of men*   Cf. *Golagros and Gawain*, 'As he is makar of man, and alkyn myght haise' 11.794.

287 *Faylid*   'Lacked', cf. *Alex B* 'And wiþ him fare as a fol · þat failde his wittus' (1.266).

288 *Allas, þe harde stoundes*   Perhaps a proverbial phrase for 'hard times'. Cf. Chaucer, *Anelida and Arcite*, 1.238.

291 *Quen þou herghedes Helle hole*   During the three days between the Crucifixion and the Resurrection Christ was thought to have descended into Hell to release all

73

those souls worthy of salvation. The judge was one of those left behind.

296 The idea of the apple as poisonous was common. Cf. *Cleanness*, where the apple 'en-poysened all peplez þat fro hem boþe.' (1.242); *Death and Liffe* 'When Eue ffell to the ffruite with ffingars white, & plucked them of the plant, & poysoned them both' (11.272-3).

298 Ze Emphasizes the judge's position outside the body of the Church.

299 Fulloght in fonte Cf. *Awntyrs of Arthur* 'Folowed in fontestone frely by-forne' (XVIII.225), *Cleanness* 'þat euer wern fulzed in font þat fest to have (1.164).

302 þe depe lake Cf. *Awntyrs of Arthur* 'Withe Lucyfer in a lake loz am I lighte' (XIII.164). *Alex B* 'þouz þei ben damned to dul · when hure day endus' (1.1111).

305 Sorow and sike Cf. *Dest. Troy* 'Soche sikyng and sorow sanke in his hert' and 'All in sikyng & sorow, with syling of teris' (.11.1515, 2680).

310 'So that all those who heard the words wept for pity.'

314 Lavande Implies a theological as well as a physical washing. O.B.Hardison, Jr. *Christian Rite and Christian Drama in the Middle Ages*, 1965, 'The washing of hands (lavabo inter innocentes) is, morally, a cleansing of the soul and is, in terms of rememorative sumbolism, the tears wept by Christ for man before the Crucifixion' (p.62). Cf. Also *Ephesians* v.26 on the effects of baptism: Ut illam sanctificaret, mundans lavacro acquae in verbo vitae.' (Quoted by Aguinas 268 art 1.).

324 Oure This is the first indication of the judge's salvation. Hitherto he has differentiated himself from those who have been baptized, but now he counts himself among the members of the Church.

325   The judge has joined the company of heaven who sing continual praises to God. Cf. *Alex A.* 'Ʒe ne herien nought herteli · þe heie god alone' (1.641). *Cleanness* 'heryd highly' (1.1527).

329 Wordes þat þou werpe   Cf. *Dest. Troy* 'and warpet these wordes, as ye wete shall' (1.2481); *Morte Arthure* 'And wysse me to werpe owte some worde at this tyme' (1.9).

337 Marcialle   The scene imagined is one of great formality, pomp, splendour. The judge is met, as an honoured guest at a feast would be, by the marshal whose duty it is to escort him to his place, according to his rank. There is a marshal at the feast in *Cleanness* (1.91).

340 ffro bale has broʒt us to blis   Cf. *Death and Liffe* 'Bringe vs into blisse, þat brought vs out of bale' (1.21). *þou* Refers to the bishop.

350 Meche mournyng & myrthe was mellyd to geder   Cf. *Golagros and Gawain*, 'Al thus with murnyng and myrth thai maid melle' (1.1148).

APPENDIX

IN 1483 WHEN William Caxton printed an English transla-
tion of the *Legenda Aurea* he added several national
saints. This Life is an epitome of the version written
by Capgrave; I have transcribed it from ULC Inc.2.d.1.1.
[3781] ff. 398vb-399vb.

Life of St. Erkenwold

And here foloweth the lyf of saint erkenwolde bysshop

Saynt erkenwolde was borne of noble lygnage/ His fader
was named offa/ and was kyng of eest englond/ and he had
also a suster named alburgh/ Whiche Erkenwolde and Al-
burgh were of right parfyte lyf/ and how be it that
theyr fader was a paynym/ yet were thyse two chyldren
crysten/ & whan erkenwolde was in parfyte age he wente
in to relygyon and was made first abbot of chirchesey/
where he lyued an holy lyf/ and after he was made
bysshop of london/ & his suster alburgh was his trewe
folower in good werkys/ and was a woman of relygyon/ and
for hir holy lyf she was made abbesse of berkynge/ Thys
holy man by thinformacion of saynt Austyn & mellyte was
enformed in the feythe in suche wyse that he vtterly
forsoke the world/ & ordeyned and buylded ii monasteryes/
one for hym selfe at chyrcheseye/ & another for hys
suster [f.399] at barkyng/ which after hir baptesme was
named ethelburga/ and saynt erkenwolde counceylled his
suster to flee worldely vanytees/ and so he dyd hym
self/ and gaue hym in to deuyne contemplacyon/ & gaue
gladly suche goodes/ as he had besyde them that he spent
in the fondacyon and buyldyng of the sayd monasteryes to
poure peple and he chaunged his erthely herytage his
worldly dygnyte/ and hys grete patrymonye in to the
herytage and lyuelode of holy chirche for to haue hys
herytage in heuen/ and he dyd al thyse expencis or he
was called to be bysshop of london/ and the holy theo-
dore archebysshop of caunterburye dyd do consecrate hym
bysshop of london/ and hys suster was sette in berkyng

with other vyrgynes for to be alweye ocupyd in the seruyce of our lord/ and it happed on a tyme as tharty-fycers that bylded the monasterye at berkynge/ were ouer seen in takyng the mesure of a pryncipal beme/ for it was to shorte & wolde not accorde to the place that it was ordeyned for/ Wherfore they made moche sorowe/ Thenne this holy man saynt erkenwolde and his suster seyng thys mysfortune/ toke the same beme bytwene theyr hondes/ and drewe it out in such wyse that it had suffycyente lengthe and accorded vnto the propre place that it was ordeyned to/ Whiche myracle was anone knowen openlye to the people/ and at that tyme were noo nonnes in englonde/ wherfore saint erkenwolde sente ouer see/ for a deuoute relygyous woman named hyldelyth to whome he bytoke his suster for to be enformed in the relygyon/ as wel in connyng/ as in good maners and vertuous doc-tryne/ in which she prouffyted in suche wyse that she passed all hir felawes in connynge/ & sone after she was made abbesse and chyef of al the monasterye/ and it happed sone after that the bysshop of london deyed whos name was cedda/ & by consente of the kynge and alle the people thys holy man of god erkenwolde/ was bysshop of london/ and what someuer he taughte in worde/ he ful-fylled it in dede/ for he was parfyte in wysedom softe and dyscrete in worde/ bysy in prayer/ chaast of body/ & hooly yeuen to goddes lore/ and was planted in the rote of charyte/ and afterward whan he had suffred moche trybulacion wyth many ghoostly batayllles/ he began to waxe ryght seek/ and thenne he commaunded to make redy his chare that he might goo and preche in the cytee the worde of god/ Wherfore it was kepte in custome longe tyme after of his dyscyples and many other to touche hym and kysse hym/ and whatsomeuer sekenesse that they had they were anone delyuerd therof/ and were made parfyt-elye hool/

In a day of somer as thys blessyd saynt/ saynt erken-wolde rode in hys chare for to preche the word of god/ It fortuned that the one whele of the chare fyl of fro the axtre/ and that notwythstondyng the chare went forth

stode vp and commaunded scylence/ and tolde to the peple
a grete commendacyon of the vertuous llyf of this holy
saynt/ and sayd it was not honest ne accordyng to
mysentrete the holy body by vyolente hondes/ but lete vs
byseche almyghty god wyth good deuocyon and mekenesse of
herte for to shewe to vs somme token by reuelacyon/ in
what place this holy body shal reste/ and alle the
people consented therto/ and knelyd doun and prayed
deuoutelye/ and whyles they were in prayer/ they sawe
that the water deuyded as it dyd to moyses in the reed
sea/ and to the chyldren goyng thorugh in to deserte/
In lyke wyse god gafe a drye path to the peple of london
for to conueye thys holy body thorugh the water to the
cytee/ and anone they toke vp the body with grete
honoure and reuerence/ and by one assente thy bare it
thorugh the pathe/ the water stondyng vp on euery syde/
and the people not wetyng theyr feet/ and so they came
to stratforde/ and sette doun the bere in a fayre mede
ful of floures/ and anone after the wedder began to wexe
fayre and clere after the tempeste/ and the tapres were
made to brenne/ wythout puttyng to fyre of ony mannes
honde/ and thus it plesyd our lord for to multeplye
myracles to thonour & worshyp of this holy saynt/ Wher-
fore the peple were full of ioye & gladnes/ & gaue lawde
to al myghty god/ & thenne they toke vp the body &
brought it to poules/ and as many seek folkes as touched
his bere were made hole/ anone as they touched the bere
of al their sekenesses/ by the merytes of the holy
bisshop saynt Erkenwolde/ & after they leyed & buryed
the body honourably in saynt Poules chirche/ where as
our lord hath shewed many a fayr myracle/ as in delyuer-
yng of prysoners out of theyr yrons seke folke to their
helth/ blynde to their syght/ and lame men to their
bodelye strengthe/ & emonge al other he hath ben a
special protectour to the sayd chirche ageynst fyre/
where on a tyme the chirche was brente/ and his shryne
which was thenne but tre was sauyd thorugh his holy
merytes/ in so moche that the clothe that laye vpon it
was not perisshed/ Another tyme whan a grete fyre had

brente a grete parte of the cyte/ & shold haue entred
vpon the chirche/ saynt erkenwolde was seen on the
chirche with a baner fyghtyng ageynst the fyre/ & so
saued and kepte his chirche fro brennyng/ Thenne lete vs
praye vnto this holy saynt that he be a special aduocate
for vs to almyghty god that we may be preserued from al
perylles of fyre & water/ & that he so gouerne vs by-
twene welth & aduersyte in this present lyf/ that we
beyng assoyled from synne & vyces/ may be brought vnto
heuenly ioye where laude honour & glorye be gy[u]en to
the blessyd trynyte wor[l]d wythouten ende amen/
  Thus endeth the lyf of saynt Erkenwolde bysshop.

GLOSSARY

THE GLOSSARY CONTAINS all forms of all words including proper names; i, y, and u, v are classed together, þ (thorn) follows t and ʒ (yogh) follows gh. Double f is treated as single f. Only the first three occurrences of common words are noted.

a, an,   indef. art. a, an, one, 3, 27, 38.

abatyd,   v. knocked down, demolished, 37.

abbay,   n. abbey, 108.

aboute,   adv. around, 48; prep. about, in connection with, 56, 110.

abyme,   n. abyss, Hell, 334.

acounte,   n. account, reckoning, 209.

Adam,   n. Adam, 295.

adoun,   adv. down, 332.

afreke,   see *freke.*

after,   adv. after (time) 112; prep. behind him, 116, 141; to attain, seek, yearn, 126, 304, 307; according to, 195; *after þat,* conj. after, 207.

afterwarde,   adv. afterward, 127.

age,   n. age, 150.

aghe,   n. awe, fear, reverence, 234.

aght,   n. eight, 210.

aght,   v. owned, 27; *aghtes,* v. owned, 224

aghtene,   n. eighteen, 208.

al, all, alle,   n. all, everything, 23, 48, 54, etc.; adj. all, 10, 14, 32, etc.; adv. completely, 75, 78, 122.

alder,   n. elder, ancestor, 295.

alder-grattest, alder-grattyst,   adj. greatest, 5, 337.

alas,   interj. alas, 288.

alowes,   v. commends, 267.

als,   adv. all as, completely, 85, 87, 89, etc.

also,   adv. also, 327, 339.

al-to-geder,   adv. altogether, completely, 228.

mon,   see *man.*

mounte,   v. extend to, 284.

an,   prep. in, 88.

and,   conj. and, 2, 3, 9, etc.

anoye, *noye*,   n. tribulation, 211, 289.

ansuare,   n. answer, 127; v. answer, 184.

any,   adj. any (implies negation), 85, 206, 284.

Appolyn,   n. Apollo, 19.

appull,   n. apple, 295.

araide, *arayed*,   v. dressed, 77, 121.

are,   adv. before, 36.

are, *arne*, *art*,   see *be*.

art,   n. district, 33.

as,   conj. as, 4, 36, 43, etc.; as if, 64, 88, 92, etc.;
    þere *as*,   when, 167; *assone*,   as soon, 345.

ask, *askyd*,   v. ask(ed), 96, 171.

aspied,   v. saw, 65.

assent,   n. assent, permission, 66.

assone,   see *as*.

at,   prep. at, 1, 34, 170, etc.

atyrid,   v. dressed, 130.

Austyn, *Augustynes*,   n. Saint Augustine('s) of Canter-
                    bury, 12, 33.

autere,   n. altar, 137.

auay,   v. inform, 174.

auisyd,   v. considered, 53.

awen,   adj. own, 235.

ay,   adv. always, 278, 287, 301; *ay-lastande*,   adj. ever-
    lasting, eternal, 347.

bad,   see *bydde*.

baythes,   v. inquires, asks, 257.

bale,   n. anguish, 257; sufferings of Hell, 340;
        balefully,   adv. sadly, 311.

bapteme,   n. baptism, 330.

barones,   n. barons, 142.

bashis,   v. dismays, 261.

be,   v. to be, 94, 97, 122, etc.; *are*, *arne*, *art*, are,
    33, 36, 164, etc.; *been*, *ben(e)*, been, 7, 26, 88;
    is, is, 19, 25, 33, etc.; *nas*, was not, 285; *wos*,
    was, was, 3, 11, 12, etc.; *were*, were, 32, 52, 53, etc.

bede, see *biddes*.

bedels, n. beadles, messengers, 59, 111.

before, prep. in front of, 149; adv. before, 209.

begynnes, v. begins, 131.

behalve, n. behalf, 181.

belle(s), n. bell(s), 117, 352.

Belyn, n. Belinus, 213.

beme, n. beam, the cross, 182.

ben, see *be*.

benche, n. bench, judge's seat, 250.

bende, v. bent, 182.

bere, v. bore, lowered, 311; gave birth to, 326.

beryd, v. resounded, 352.

Berynge, n. Brennius, 213.

besyde, prep. beside, 142.

besiet, v. busied, 56.

best, adv. best, 272.

bete(n), v. beat(en), conquered, 9; struck, pulled
                  down, 37.

better, adv. better, 18.

bi, *by*, prep. by, 90; near, beside, 32, 72; *byside*,
                  beside, 67.

bydde, *biddes*, v. bids, 181, 221; *bede*, 67; offered,
                  243; *boden*, offered, 214.

bigriped, v. gripped, surrounded, 80.

byhoues, v. behoves, 168.

biknowe, v. reveal, 221.

bileve, n. belief, 173, 299.

bischop, *byschop*, *bisshop*, *byšschop*, n. bishop, 3, 33,
                                         105, etc.

biseche, v. beseech, 120.

bitan, v. given, 28.

bitwene, prep. between, 196, 214.

blakke, adj. black, 343.

blee, n. complexion, appearance, 87; condition, 343.

blessid, *blessyd*, *blissid*, v. blessed, 3, 326, 340.

blynne, v. to cease, 111.

blis(se), n. blis, salvation, 340, 345; *blisful(l)*,
                  adj. blissful, blessed, 76, 326.

blysnande, adj. gleaming, 87.
blo, adj. livid, ash-coloured, 290.
blode, n. blood, 182, 290.
blonke, n. horse, 112.
bode, *boode*, n. bidding, command, 181, 193; *bodeword*, message, 105.
boden, see *bidde*.
body, n. body, 76, 94, 106, etc.
boghe, v. bow, submit to, 194.
boghit, v. approached, 59.
boghtes, v. bought, redeemed, 289.
boke, n. book, 103.
bolde, adj. bold, courageous, 213; great, excellent, 106
bone, n. petition, 194; adj. ready, 181.
bone, n. killer, 243.
bones, n. bones, 346.
bonkes, n. banks, 32.
bordure(s), n. border(s), 51, 82.
bot, adv. only, 32, 208; conj. but, 52, 54, 73, etc.; that, 97; unless, 158; *I may not but*, I can only, 194.
bote, n. profit, good, benefit, 170; relief, 327.
bothe, adj. both, 194.
bothum, n. bottom, floor, deepest part, 76.
bounty, n. goodness, virtue; *bounty my body*, as a reward, 248.
bourne, n. stream, 330.
brawnche, n. branch, a small share, 276.
brayed, v. wept, 190.
Bretaynes, n. Britain's, 32; *Breton(s)*, Briton(s), 9, 213.
brevyt, v. reported, 103.
bryȝt, adj. bright, shining, 51, 87, 190.
brynge, v. bring, 56; *broght*, *broȝt*, brought, 9, 105, 340
brode, adj. broad, *crownes ful brode*, tonsures, 55.
brothir, n. brother, 213.
Brutus, Brutus, legendary founder of British race, 207.
buggid, *buggyd*, v. built, 37, 207.
burde, v. ought, 260.

burgeys, n. burgesses, 59.
burghe, n. town, city, 3, 103, 207, etc.
buried, *buriet*, v. buried, 94, 248; adj. buried, 106.
burynes, n. tomb, 142, 190.
buskyd, v. hastened, 112.
busmare, n. insult, 214.

caȝt, v. caught, 148.
callid, v. called, 16.
camelyn, n. a fabric of wool mixed with silk or other fibres, 82.
careless, adj. generous, 172.
carpe, v. recite, 317.
cast, v. cast, sprinkle (water), 317.
cause, n. cause, 221; *causes*, n. legal charges, 202.
caysere, n. emperor, 199.
cenacle, n. dining room, specifically the upper chamber where the apostles gathered, 336.
cessyd, v. ended, 136, 341.
chargit, v. bound by oath, 18.
chaungit, v. changed, 18.
chere, n. face, 342.
chevely, adv. first of all, promptly, 18.
childes, n. Christ's, 318.
cite, n. city, 202.
cladden, v. clad, clothed, 249.
clansyd, v. cleansed, purified, 16.
clene, adj. clean, 82, 259.
clerke, n. clerk, canon, 55.
clos, n. Cathedral close, 55.
cloth(e)(s), n. cloth, clothes, 82, 148, 259, etc.
cloutes, n. shreds, 259.
cloyster, n. cloister, 140.
clustered, adj. gathered in a cluster, 140.
colde, adv. distressingly, 305.
colour(e), n. colour, 263; complexion, 148.
comaundit, v. commanded, 115.
come, v. come, 74; came, 113, 142; *commen*, came, 63.
comforthe, n. comfort, 168, 172.

committed, v. put in charge, 201.
communates, n. members of the community, the people, 14.
con, v. can, 156; *couthe*, could, 100, 101, 249.
confirmyng, v. confirming, 124.
confourmyd, v. conformed, 242.
consciens, n. conscience, 237.
conuertyd, v. converted, 14.
corce, *cors*, n. corpse, 110, 177, 317.
corners, n. corners, 71.
coron, *croun*, n. crown, 83, 222; *coronyd*, v. crowned,
          254.
corrupt, v. putrified, 346.
councele, v. conceal, 184.
counsell, n. counsel, 167, 172, 266.
courte, n. court, 249.
couthe, see *con*.
couthely, adv. plainly, clearly, 98.
couert, v. covered, 346.
couetise, n. covetousness, 237.
coyfe, n. coif, judge's headdress, 83.
crafte, n. skill, 167, 346; *crafty*, adj. learned, 44.
crakit, v. was uttered, spoken of, 110.
creatore, n. creator, God, 168.
creatures, n. creature's, man's, 167.
cry, n. cry, 110.
Crist(e)(s), n. Christ('s), 2, 16, 209; *Cristen*, adj.
          Christian, 124, 209; *Cristendame*, *Cristen-
          dome*, n. Christendom, 2, 14.
cronecles, *cronicle*, n. chronicle(s), 44, 156.
crosse, n. cross, 2.
croun, see *coron*.
crowes, n. crowbars, 71.
crownes, n. tonsures, 55.
cumly, adj. comely, handsome, 82.
cure, n. responsibility, 168.
curtest, adj. most couteous, 249.

dalf, v. delved, dug, 45; *doluen*, adj. dug down, 99.
dampned, v. damned, 302.

date, n. date, 205.

daungerde, v. endangered, put in jeopardy, 320

dawes, n. days, 7; *day(es)*, day(s), 117, 155, 180; v. dawns, 306; *dawid*, dawned, 127.

debonerte, n. humility, modesty, kindness, 123.

declynet, v. declined, strayed, turned aside, 237.

dede, n. deed, 169, 301.

dede, adj. dead, 225, 309; abs. adj. dead man, 116.

dedifie(t), v. dedicate(d), 6, 23.

deere, dere, adj. dear, precious, 23, 123, 144; *derrest*, most dear, 29.

defaute, n. blemish, 148.

deghed, v. died, 246.

dene, n. dean, 144.

denyed, v. resounded, 246.

depe, adv. deep, 45, 99; adj. deep, 302.

deputate, n. deputy, 227.

derfe, adj. difficult, 99.

derke, adj. dark, 117, 294, 306.

deth(e), n. death, 247; *derke deth*, damnation, Hell, 294, 306.

deuel(l), n. devil, 15, 27.

deuyse, v. consider, 225; *deuisyt*, described, 144; reflected upon, 309.

deuoydes, v. avoids, escapes, 348; *deuoydit*, shunned, 116.

deuyne, v. speculate, guess, 169.

dight, diȝt, v. dug, 45; brought about, 294; prepared, 23.

digne, v. grant, 123.

dynly, adv. dimly, gloomily, 306.

ditte, v. did, shut, 116.

dyuerse, adj. diverse, 60.

do, v. do, 169.

dole, part, section, 6.

doluen, see *dalfe*.

dome, n. judgment, sentence, 236; *domesmon*, n. judge, 227.

Domini, see *Spiritus*.

dores, n. doors, 128.

doun, adv. down, 6, 37, 311, etc.

drawen, v. pulled down, 6.

drede, n. dread, fear, 233.

dreme, n. voice, speaking; *wyt a drery dreme*, speaking mournfully, 191.

drery, adj. see *dreme*.

dresse, v. make, deliver, 236.

dryghten, n. lord, god, 29.

dryues, v. pushes, forces, 191.

drofe, see *ouer*.

droppyd, v. dropped, 320.

duke, n. duke, 227.

dul, n. mourning, grief, 246; *dulfully*, adv. mournfully, 302, 309.

durre, n. door, 116.

dwellid, v. dwelled, lived, 10.

dwynande, v. languishing, 294.

efte, adv. once again, 37.

eggit, adj. having a cutting edge; *eggit toles*, tools or instruments with cutting blade, 40.

egh, n. eye; *egh lyddes*, eyelids, 178; *eghen*, eyes, 194, 311, 321.

elles, adv. in a different way, 121.

embawmyd, *enbawmyd*, v. embalmed, 261, 265.

enbelicit, v. embellished, decorated, 51.

ende, n. end; *later ende*, concluding part, 136.

Englond, n. England, 1.

enioynyd, v. appointed, 216.

enprise, n. enterprise, undertaking, 253.

entouchid, v. poisoned, 297.

er(e), adv. before, 19, 24, 118.

eres, n. ears, 90.

Erkenwalde, *Erkenwolde*, n. Erkenwald, 4, 33, 108, etc.

erth(e), n. earth, ground, 45; the world, 196, 198, 237.

Esex, n. Essex, 108.

ete, v. ate, 295.

euel, adv. hardly, 276.

euer, adv. ever, 103, 104, 110, etc.; *euermore*, always, 26.
exilid, v. exiled, excluded, 303.

face, n. face, 89, 323.
fader, n. father, 244, 294; father's, 243.
faylid, v. failed, lacked, 287; vanished, 342.
fayne, adj. happy, eager, 176.
fair(e), adj. handsome, 46, 317.
faith(e), *fayth(e)*, n. faith, Christianity, 13, 124;
          belief, 173, 204, 242; *faitheful*, adv. accord-
          ing to doctrine, 299; *faitheles*, adj. without
          Christianity, 287.
fals, adj. false, deceitful, 231; corrupt, dishonest, 244.
fastynge, n. fastening, securing, 173.
fauour, n. favour, 244.
fell, v. befell, 244.
felle, v. fell, 323.
felonse, adj. felonous, wicked, 231.
ferforthe, adv.; *als ferforthe as*, just as much as, 242.
ferly, n. wonder, 46; adj. strange, 145.
fest, n. feast, 303.
fife, adj. five, 208.
fynde, v. find, 156; *fyndynge*, n. discovery, 145.
fyne, adj. faithful, pure, 173; *fynest*, supreme, 252.
fynger, n. finger, 145, 165.
fyrre, n. end, 293; adv. further, 169.
ffirst, *fyrst(e)*, adv. first, 42, 144, 197.
fflesh, n. flesh, skin, 89.
flore, n. floor, 46.
folke, n. folk, people, 231.
folowid, v. followed, 351.
folwe, v. baptise, 318.
fonte, n. baptismal font, 299.
ffor, conj. for, because, 7, 29, 45, etc.; prep. for,
        38, 40, 41, etc.
forgo, v. abandon, forsake, 276.
forthe, adv. forth, out, 351.
fforþi, conj. therefore, 279.
forto, part. to, 298.

forwrast, adj. wrested away (from themselves), spell-
        bound, 220.

fote, n. base, 42.

founden, v. found, discovered, 43, 46.

fourme, n. form, essence, 230.

fourmyt, v. formed, 46.

fourty, adj. forty, 230.

fre, adj. noble, generous, 318.

freke, n. man, 323.

frende, n. friend, 176.

freshe, adj. fresh, 89.

fro, *ffro*, prep. from, 12, 107, 116.

frowarde, adj. unruly, disobedient, 231.

ful, *fful*, *full*, adv. very, 1, 53, 55, etc.

fulfille, v. fulfil, satisfy, 176.

fulloght, n. Baptism, 299.

fulsen, v. assist, enable, 124.

fundement, n. foundation, 42.

furrit, *ffurrid*, v. trimmed with fur, 81; covered with
        fur, 252.

gay, adj. elegant, richly attired, 75, 134.

gargeles, n. gargoyles, 48.

garnysht, v. decorated, 48.

gate, n. path; *heghe gate*, main thoroughfare, way of
        right or justice, 241.

geder, see *to*.

gedrid, v. gathered, assembled, 134.

gefe, v. gave, 282.

gentil, adj. pagan, 216, 229.

gete, v. got, 241.

gyfe, v. give, 276.

gynful, adj. crafty, treacherous, 238.

gynge, n. retinue, household, 137.

glent, v. deviate, 241.

glisnande, adj. glistening, 78.

glode, n. space, surface, 75.

glorie, n. worldly honour; *vayne glorie*, empty glory, 348.

glotte, n. filth, 297.

glowe, v. cry; *glow...opon*, pray to, 171

God(de), n. God, 171, 282, 325; *Goddis*, God's, 316.

gode, adj. good, 230.

golde, adj. gold, 24, 51; n. gold, 75, 78, 80, etc.

goste, n. soul, spirit, 192; *Holy Goste*, third member of the Trinity, 127, 319.

gouernour, n. governor, judge, 251.

gowne, n. gown, 78.

grace, n. God's grace, 120, 126, 171; *gracious*, adj. merciful, 319.

graunte, n. grant, assurance, 126.

graue, n. grave, 153.

gray, adj. grey, 48.

graythist, adj. most skilled, truest, 251.

grete, adj. great, mighty, 134, 141, 282, etc.

grete, n. earth, 41.

grette, v. lamented, sought, 126.

gronyng, n. sigh of lamentation, 282.

grounde, n. ground, 41.

grubber, n. digger, 41.

grue, n. a bit; *not one grue*, not a bit, 319.

gurden, v. clothed, 251.

gurdill, n. girdle, belt, 80.

ʒe(e), *ʒow*, pron. you, 170, 174, 175, etc.; *ʒour*, your, 173, 176, 209, etc.

ʒea, interj. yes, 273.

ʒemyd, v. ruled, looked after, 202.

ʒere(s), n. year(s), 11, 208, 210.

ʒet, adv. still, 44, 148, 257; even, 199; more, 210.

ʒistur-day, n. yesterday, 88.

ʒode, v. went, 198.

ʒorde, n. yard, 88.

ʒoskyd, v. sobbed, 312.

had(e)(n), v. had, 7, 8, 17, etc.; *haddes*, had, 224, 315; *han*, have, 300; *has*, has, 26, 98, 147, etc.; *haue*, have, 155, 260.

halde(s), *heldes*, v. hold, 42, 166, 196; *vp halden*, v. upheld, praised, 349.

halowes, n. saints, 23.
harde, adj. hard, 40; painful, 288.
harmes, n. damages, pain, sorrow, 232.
hathel, n. man, 198.
hatte, v. was called, 4, 25, 38.
he, pron. he, 13, 15, 17, etc.
hedde, n. head, 281.
heere, v. praise, 339; *herid*, praised, 325.
heghe, adj. high, 129, 223, 325, etc.; *highest*, highest, noblest, 253; *heghe gate*, see *gate*; *heghe gynge*, noble company, 137.
heire, n. heir, 211.
heldes, see *haldes*.
heldyt, v. went, 137.
helle, n. Hell, 196, 291, 307.
hemmyd, v. decorated with an ornamental border, perhaps fringed, 78.
hende, adj. noble, 58; merciful, 325.
Hengyst, n. Hengist's, 7.
hent, v. received, suffered, 232; *hents*, removed, 291.
herden, v. heard, 310.
here, adv. here, 13, 146, 147, etc.
herghedes, v. plundered; *herghedes Helle hole*, harrowed Hell, 291.
herken, v. listen to, 134; *herken after*, v. desire, 307.
hert, n. heart, 242, 257.
hethen, adj. heathen, 7.
heuen, n. heaven, 166, 196.
hew(e), v. hew, 40, 47.
hewes, n. colours, 87.
hyder, adv. hither, here, 8.
highid, v. went, 58.
him, *hym*, pron. him, 17, 100, 109, etc.
hyr, pron. its, 280, 308, etc.
his, pron. his, 5, 28, 30, etc.
hit, pron. it, 7, 26, 31, etc.
ho, pron. it, 274, 279, 308, etc.
holde, v. hold, keep, 232; contain, 249.
hole, n. hole; *Helle hole*, Hell, 291, 307.

94

holy, adj. holy, 4, 127, 319.

hom, pron. them, 9, 16, 18, etc.

home, n. home, 107.

honde(s), n. hand(s), 84, 90, 166, etc.; *honde quile*, a moment, 64.

honeste, n. honesty, 253.

hongyt, v. hanged, 244.

honour, n. honour, 253.

hope, v. believe, 4.

hor, pron. their, 17, 18, 61, etc.

houre, n. hour, time, 326.

houres, n. canonical hours, the prayers appropriate to them, 119.

how, adv. how, 95, 147, 187, etc.

hummyd, v. murmured, moaned, 281.

hundred, hundrid, adj. hundred, 58, 208.

hungride, v. hungered, sought, 304; *hungrie*, adj. hungry, 307.

hurlyd, v. hurled, 17.

I, pron. I, 4, 36, 122, etc.

Iames, n. St. James, 22.

iapes, n. frauds, 238.

ydols, n. idol(s), 17, 29.

yepely, adv. cunningly, quickly, 88.

Iesu, n. Jesus, 22, 180.

yet, conj. yet, 148.

if, conj. if, 176, 271, 274.

ylka, ilke, adj. same, 101, 193; each, 96.

in, hyn, prep. in, 1, 3, 5, etc.

ioly, adj. vigorous, youthful, 229.

Iono, n. Juno, 22.

ioy, n. the perfect joy of heaven, 180, 188.

ioyned, v. appointed, assigned, 188.

yrnes, n. irons, 71.

is, see *be*.

Iubiter, n. Jupiter, 22.

iuge, n. judge, 216.

iugement, n. judgment, decision, 238.

iuggid, iuggit, v. condemned, 188; assigned, 180.
iustifiet, v. administered justice, 229.
iustises, n. judges, 254.

kaghten, v. caught, 71.
keies, n. keys, 140.
kene, adj. stalwart, 254.
kenely, adv. very much, 63.
kenne, v. to make known, 124.
kepten, v. kept, guarded, 66; *kepyd,* kept, 266.
kest, v. cast, placed, 83.
kidde, kydde, v. to make known; *kidde for,* acknowledged as, 222; recalled, 44; *kydde of,* known as, 113; adj. acknowledged, recognized, noble, 254.
kynde, n. nature; *by kynde,* according to nature, normally, 157.
kyng(e), n. king, 98, 156, 199.
kynned, v. was born, 209.
kynnes, n. kinds, 209.
kirke(s), n. church(es), 16, 113.
kith, n. country, kingdom, 98.
know(e), v. know, 74, 263; *knewe,* knew, 285.
knyʒt, n. knight, 199.

lacche, v. obtain, 316.
laddes, n. lads, boys, 61.
lady, n. lady; *Oure Lady,* the Virgin Mary, 21.
laften, v. left, 61; *laftes,* left, 292.
lagh(e)(s), lawe(s), n. law(s), 34, 187, 200, etc.
laited, v. searched, 155.
lay, v. place, lay, 67, 281, 314; *laide, layde,* laid, 72, 149; *layn(e),* lain, 95, 157, 179; *lies, ligges lye(s),* lies, 99, 179, 186; *lyggid,* lay, 76; *lying,* lying, 205.
lake, n. lake, Hell, 302.
lant, v. granted, 272; adj. lent, 192.
large, adj. large, 72.
lasse, abs. adj. the least degree, 104, 247; adv. little, 320.
lasshit, v. struck, 334.

96

last, v. last, 264, 272; *lastyd*, lasted, 215.
later, adj. concluding, 136.
lathe, v. invite (to a meal), 308.
lauande, adj. cleansing, 314.
lede, n. man, 146, 150, 200.
lege, adj. liege; *lege men*, liegemen, 224.
lely, adv. loyally, 268.
leme, n. flash of light, 334.
lene, v. grant, 315.
lenger, adv. longer, 179, 319.
lengthe, n. length, 205.
lengyd, v. dwelled, stayed, 68.
lenyd, v. lain, 328.
lepen, v. leaped, hurried, 61.
lere, *lyre*, n. face, complexion, 95, 149.
leste, adj. least, 162.
lethe, v. cease, 347.
lettes, v. prevents, stops, 165.
lettres, n. letters, 51; messages, 111.
leue, *leues*, *leuen*, v. believe(s), 175, 176, 183, etc.
lewid, adj. unknown(?), forgotten (?), 205.
librairie, n. library, 155.
liche, *lyche*, n. fellow, peer, 314; man, 146; *lykhame*,
            man, 179.
lidde, *lydde*, n. lid, 67, 72; *egh lyddes*, eyelids, 178.
life, *lyf(e)*, *lyue*, n. life, 150, 192, 224, etc.; *lyuye*,
            live, 298.
lyftand, v. lifting, 178.
lighten, v. landed, 322.
liȝtly, adv. instantly, 334.
lym, n. limb, 224.
Limbo, n. Limbo, 292.
lippes, n. lips, 91.
listonde, v. listened, 219.
litell(e), adv. little, 160, 165, 190, etc.
lo, interj. lo, behold, 146.
lodely, adj. loathsome, 328.
loffynge, n. loving, 292.
lofte, adv. above; *o lofte, on loft*, above, aloft, 49, 81.

logh(e), adv. low, 334; *on logh*, below, 147.
loke, v. look, 68, 157; *lokyd*, looked, 313.
loken, adj. locked up, 147.
lome, n. vessel, 69, 149.
londe(s), n. land(s), 30, 200, 224.
London, n. London, 1, 25, 34.
long(e), adv. long, 1, 95, 97, etc.
longen, v. belong, 268.
Lord(e), n. Lord, God, 123, 134, 175, etc.; *lords*,
     temporal lords, 138, 146.
lore, n. skill, craft, 264.
louse, *loused*, v. loose(d), 165, 178.
loue, adj. beloved, 34; *loues*, v. loves, 268, 272, 349;
     lovid, *lovyd*, loved, 288, 324.
louyng, n. praising, 349.
lures, n. perdition, 328.
luste, v. pleases, 162.

macers, n. mace-bearers, 143.
maghty, *maȝti*, *maȝty*, *myȝty*, adj. mighty, 27, 143, 175,
     etc.; *myȝt*, *myȝtes*, *myghtes*, n. strength(s),
     162, 163, 283, etc.
Mahon, n. Mohammed, any devil, 20.
may, v. may, 151, 175, 194, etc.; *myȝt*, might, 74, 94,
     97.
maire, *mayre*, n. mayor, 65, 143.
mayster, adj. master, 26, 201; *mesters*, n. master's, 60.
maystrie, n. mastery, 234.
make, v. make, 206, 238; *makyd*, *makkyd*, *made*, made, 39,
     43, 50; *maker*, n. creator, God, 283.
malte, v. melt, 158.
man, *mon*, n. man, 4, 60; *men*, men, 58, 69, 125, etc.;
     monnes, man's, 163, 234, 240; *monlokest*, adj.
     manliest, 250.
manas, n. menace, 240.
manerly, adv. well-conducted, seemly, 131.
maners, n. manners, modes of life, 60.
mantel, n. mantle, 81, 250.
marbre, n. marble, 48, 50.

marciall, n. marshall, 337.
Margrete, n. St. Margaret, 20.
martilage, n. commemorative list of dead members of the
            community, 154.
mason, n. mason, 39.
masse, n. mass, 129, 131.
matens, n. Matins, 128.
matyd, v. check-mated, stale-mated, 163.
Maudelayne, n. Mary Magdalene, 20.
me, pron. me, 124, 193, 195, etc.
meche, adj. much, 206, 220, 350; great, 81; *mecul*, adj.
        great, 27, 286.
mede(s), n. meed, reward, 234, 270.
medecyn, n. medicine, 298.
meeles, n. meals, fig. salvation, 307.
meer, n. mare, 114.
meynye, n. household, retinue, 65.
mekest, adj. meekest, most humble, 250.
mellyd, v. mixed, 350.
memorie, n. memory, 44, 158.
mendyd, v. mended, healed, 298.
mene, v. mean, 54; imagine, 151; *menyd*, lamented, 247.
menyuer, n. miniver fur, 81.
menske, n. courtesy, dignity, honour, 337; *menskefully*,
        adv. gracefully; *menskes*, v. honours, 269;
        menskid, honoured, 258.
mercy, n. mercy, 284, 286; *merciles*, adv. without mercy,
        300.
mery, adj. merry, cheerful, 39.
meritorie, adj. serving to earn reward, 270.
merkid, v. marked, 154.
meruaile, *meruayle*, n. marvel, wonder, 43, 65, 114, etc.
meschefe, n. misfortune, 240.
mesters, see *mayster*.
mesure, n. prescribed quantity, 286.
metely, adv. fittingly, suitably, 50.
metropol, ' n. metropolis, 26.
mette(n), v. met, 114, 337.
my, pron. my, 23, 184, 197.

mydell, n. middle, waist, 80.

myn, pron. mine, 194, 235, 242, etc.

mynde, n. mind, 97, 163; memory, 151, recollection, remembrance, 154; *mynnyd*, v. remembered, 104; *mynnyng*, remembering, 269.

mynyd, v. mined, 43.

ministres, n. ministers, attendants, 131.

mynster, n. church, cathedral, 27, 35, 128.

mynte, v. pointed, 145.

myrthe, *murthe*, n. joy, mirth, 335, 350.

myself, pron. myself, 300.

myste, v. missed, 300.

mysterie, n. mystery, 125.

mo, adj. more, 210.

modir, n. mother, 325.

moght-freten, adj. broken into pieces by moths, 86.

molde, n. earth, world, 270; *moldes*, earth of a grave, ashes, 343.

mony, adj. many, 11, 39, 41, etc.; abs. adj. 53, 63, 114, etc.

more, adj. more, 230, 341; *euermore*, adv. increasingly, 110; *more ne less*, *more and the lasse*, n.p. everyone, 104, 247; *most*, adv. most, 269.

morowen, morning, 306.

motes, n. dust, spots, 86.

moulyng, n. mould, 86.

mountes, v. amounts, 160.

mournyng, n. mourning, 350.

mouthe, n. mouth, 54.

muset, v. pondered; *muset hit to mouthe*, pondered over aloud, 54.

nakyd, adj. naked, uncovered, 89.

name, *nome(s)*, n. name(s), 16, 18, 28, etc.

nas, see *be*.

nattyd, v. recited, repeated, 119.

nay, interj. no, 265.

ne, conj. nor, 103, 234, 244, etc.; adj. 102, 149, 152, etc.; adv. 103, 218.

neuenyd, v. named, 25, 195.

neuer, adv. never, 156, 166, 199; *neuer so large*, as large as might be, 72; *neuer so riche*, as rich as might be, 72, 239.

new(e), adv. anew, again, 6, 14, 37; adj. new, 25, 35, 211.

nyȝt, n. night, 117, 119.

no, adj. no, 148, 159, 169, etc.; adv. 179, 234, 238, etc.

noble, adj. noble, 38, 227.

noght, noȝt, n. nothing, 56, 101; adv. not at all, 261; *noȝt full*, not very, 1; only, 208.

noice, noyce, n. noise, 62, 218.

nommbre, n. number, 206, 289.

non, adv. not, 157, 289; *non(e)*, n. no one, 101, 241.

nones, n. nonce; *for þe nones*, for the purpose, 38.

not, adv. not, 74, 97, 185.

note, n. thing, work, 38, 101.

note, n. mark, sign, 152; *notes*, n. musical notes, 133.

nothyre, noþir, adv. neither, 102, 152, 199.

notyd, v. noted down, 103.

nourne(t), v. express, explain, 101; belong to, 152; conjured, 195.

now, adv. now, 19, 25, 169, etc.; conj. now, 33, 179.

noy, n. see *anoye*.

o, part. on; *o lofte*, aloft, above, 49; *on*, prep. on, upon, 2, 42, 46, etc.

of, prep. of, 19, 21, 24, etc.

ofte, adv. often, 135, 232.

one, adj. one, 6, 152, 156, etc.; n. one, 214.

ones, adv. once, 352.

openly, adv. openly, uncovered, 90.

opon, prep. upon, 76, 92, 125, etc.

or, conj. or, 121.

othir, oþer, oþir, pron. other, 32, 59, 93; adj. 346; adv. either, 86, 188, 255; conj. either, 86.

our, pron. our, 154, 155, 169, etc.; *Oure Lady*, the Virgin Mary, 21.

out(e), owt(e), adv. out, 9, 17, 158, etc.

outen, see *wyt*.

ouer, adv. over, past, 117; *ouer drofe*, rushed past, 117.

payne, n. pain, 333.
payntyd, v. painted, 75.
paynym(es), n. pagan(s), 203, 285.
palais, n. palace, 115.
paradis, n. paradise, 161.
parage, n. high lineage, noble rank, 203.
partyd, v. departed, 107.
passid, *passyd*, v. passed (by), 115, 138, 141, etc.
Paule, n. Paul, 35, 113.
pepul(l), n. people, 10, 109, 217, etc.
perle, n. pearl, 79.
peruertyd, v. corrupted, 10.
pes, n. peace, 115.
Petre, n. Peter, 19.
picchit, v. fastened, 79.
pinchid, v. squeezed, pressed, 70.
pyne, n. pain, 141; torment, 188.
place, n. place, 10, 144, 153, etc.
playn, n. open space, 138.
planed, v. planed, finished smoothly, 50.
plantyd, v. planted, 13.
plied, v. attended, bowed, 138.
plyȝtles, adj. unpledged, 296.
plite, n. pledged, 285.
poysned, n. poisoned, damned, 296.
pontificals, n. vestments and other insignia of a
              bishop, 130.
pope, n. pope, 12.
porer, abs. adj. poorer (people), 153.
powder, n. powder, 344.
power, n. power, 228.
praysid, v. praised, worshipped, 29.
prece, n. press, crowd, 141.
prechyd, v. preached, 13.
precious, adj. precious, 79.
prelacie, n. order or rank of prelates, 107.

prelate, n. bishop, 130, 138.
prestly, adv. promptly, 130.
primate, n. archbishop, here the bishop of London, 107.
prince, n. prince, 161, 203.
prises, n. levers, 70.
procession, n. procession, 351.
Providens, n. Providence, 161.
Psalmyde, adj. sung; *psalmyde writtes*, psalms, 277.
pure, adj. pure, true, 13.
putte(n), v. put, 70, 153, 228.

quaynt, adj. elegant, 133.
quat, adj. what, 94, 186, 187; adv. what, 301; pron. what, 68; inter. pron. what, 54.
queme, adj. pleasant, 133.
quen(e), inter. adv. when, 57, 65, 128.
quere, rel. adv. where, 274, 279.
quere, n. choir, 133.
questis, n. baying (of dogs); long and deep notes, 133.
queþer, inter. conj. whether, if, 188; adversative conj. although, 153.
quy, adv. why, 186, 222, 223.
quil(e), n. while, time, 105; *hond quile*, a moment, 64; conj. while, 215, 217.
quo, pron. who, 185, 197.
quontyse, n. skill, ingenuity, strange thing, 74.
quoth, v. said, 146, 159, 193.

radly, adv. quickly, immediately, 62.
raght, *raȝt*, v. reached, gave, 256, 280, 338.
rattes, n. rags, scraps, 260.
rayked, v. proceeded, 139.
reame, n. realm, 11, 135.
rede, adj. red, 91.
redeless, adj. without counsel, helpless, 164; *redy*, wise, prudent, 245.
redes, v. governs, 192.
refetyd, v. refreshed with food, 304.
regne, n. reign, 212; *regnyd*, v. reigned, 151.
reken(est), adj. straightforward, upright, 135, 245.

relefe, n. relief, 328.

remewit, v. removed, strayed, 235.

renaide, adj. apostate, renegade, 11.

renk(e)(s), n. man, men, 239, 271, 275.

rent, v. rent, torn, 260.

repairen, v. go, went, 135.

reson, n. reason, rationality, 267; cause, 235; *resons,* n. explanation, 164; *resones,* n. sentences, 52.

restorement, n. restoration, restitution, 280.

reule, v. to rule, 331; *rewlit,* v. ruled, 212.

reuele, v. reveal, 121.

reuerence, n. reverence, a bow, 338; *reuerens,* reverence, 239.

reuestid, v. dressed to celebrate the mass, 139.

rewardes, rewardid, v. reward(ed), judge(d), 256, 275.

riall, adj. royal, 77.

rich(e), adj. rich, noble, 77, 83, 212; adv. richly, nobly, 139; *richely,* richly, 304.

right, riȝt, ryȝt, riȝtes, n. right, righteousness, 232, 235, 241, etc.; *ryȝtwys,* adj. righteous, 245.

ryngand, v. ringing, 62; *ronge,* v. rang, 117.

rises, v. rises, 344.

ryue, n. tear, 262.

rode, n. ruddy, 91; n. rood, the cross, 290.

roynyshe, adj. indecipherable, 52.

ronke, adj. rebellious, 11; abundant, 91, 262.

ronnen, v. ran, 62.

rose, n. rose, 91.

roten, adj. rotten, 344; *rotid,* v. rotted, 260.

rottok, n. a decayed or musty thing, 344.

route, n. assembly, in a body, 62.

route, n. rot, 262.

routhe, n. ruth, pity, 240.

row, n. row, in a line, 52.

rowme, n. room, place, 338.

sacrid, sacryd, v. consecrated, 3, 159.

sacrifices, n. sacrifices, 30.

sadde, adj. sad, 324.

safe, see *vouchsafe*.

saynt(es), n. saint(s), 12, 17, 19, etc.

sake, n. sake, 239.

same, adj. same, 204.

Sandewiche, n. Sandwich, 12.

Sathanas, n. Satan, 24.

saule, soule, n. soul, 273, 279, 293, etc.

sauyoure, n. saviour, 324.

sawe, n. decree, command, 184.

Saxon(es), n. Saxon(s), 8, 24, 30.

say(d)(e), say(e)s, v. say, 100, 122, 136, etc.; *sayd causes*, trials, 202.

sayntuare, n. sactuary, holy places, 166.

schedde, v. shed, 182; *sheddes*, sheds, 329.

se, v. see, 170, 293, 308.

seche, v. seek, search, 41, 170.

sege, n. seat, see, 35.

segge, n. man, 100, 159, 189, etc.

sele, n. good fortune, 279.

selfe, pron. self, *my self*, 197; *oure selfe*, ourselves, 170; *þi selven*, thyself, you, 185.

semely, adj. handsome, appropriate, 84; adv. decorously, 35.

semes, v. seems, 98.

send(e), v. sent, 8, 12, 111; *sende*, send, 172.

sene, v. seen, 100.

septre, septure, n. sceptre, 84, 223, 256.

ser, pron. sir, 225.

seruice, n. service, mass, 136.

seruyd, v. served, 275.

sesyd, v. seized, *sesyd in*, to be the legal possessor, 345.

sett, v. allotted, dedicated, 21, 24; set, 84; *sette*, v. placed, 332.

seuen, n. seven, 155.

sewid, v. followed, 204.

sextene, n. sexton, 66.

shapen, v. shaped, fashioned, 88.

sike, v. sigh, 305; *syked*, sighed, 189, 323.

synagoge, n. pagan temple, 21.

synge, v. sing, 129.

sit, sitte, v. sit, judge, 202, 305; *syttes, sittes*, sits, 35, 293.

sithen, sythen, conj. since, 2, 180, 185, etc.; adv. *longe sythen*, long ago, 1, 260.

skelton, v. hasten, 278.

skilfulle, abs. adj. rational, one who does right, 278.

slekkyd, v. slaked, relieved, 331.

slent, n. splash, sprinkle, 331.

slepe, n. sleep, 92.

slippid, v. slipped, 92.

slode, v. slid, 331.

so, conj. so, 23, 169; adv. so, 45, 63, 72, etc.

sodanly, sodenly, adv. suddenly, 92, 342.

solemply, adv. solemnly, 129; ceremoniously, 336; *solempne*, adj. ceremonious, 303; *solempnest*, most serious, important, 30.

sone, adv. soon, quickly, 58, 72.

songen, v. sung, 128.

sonne, n. sun, 21.

soper, n. supper, 303, 308, 332; *soupen*, v. sup, eat, 336.

sorow(e), n. sorrow, 305, 309, 327.

sothe, soþe, n. truth, 159, 170, 197; adj. true, 277.

soule, see *saule*.

soun, n. sound, 324; *sowne*, n. report, tidings, 341; *sounde*, n. swoon, 92.

souerayn, n. sovereign, 120.

space, n. space, room, 93; time, 312.

spakly, adv. hastily, 312, 335.

speche, n. speech, language, 152; *speke*, v. speak, 312; *spake*, spoke, 217.

spede, n. speed, success, 132; *spedeless*, adj. unsuccessful, ineffectual, 93.

spelunke, n. cave, cavern, or grotto; tomb, 49, 217.

sperl, n. bars, bolts, 49.

Spiritus Domini, n. Holy Spirit, 132.

spradde, v. spread; *spradde hit o lofte,* extended it
        above, 49.
sprange, v. sprang, 217.
sprent, v. sprinted, sprang, 335.
spyr, v. ask, 93.
spyrit, n. soule, 335.
stablid, stablyd, v. established, 2; installed, 274.
stadde, v. fixed, placed, 274.
stille, adv. still, 219.
ston(es), n. stone(s), 40, 47, 219.
stondes, v. stands, 164; *stode,* stood, 97; *stoden,*
        stood, 52, 73, 219.
stoundes, n. times; *þe harde stoundes,* time of tribula-
        tion, 288.
strange, adj. strange, 74.
streʒt, adv. straight, righteously, 274.
such(e), dem. adj, such, 97, 104, 110, etc.
suffrid, v. suffered, 2.
sum(me), adj. some, 100, 192, 276.
sutile, adj. wise, penetrating, 132.
swarues, v. deviates, errs, 167.
swete, adj. sweet, 120; pleasing, 342.
swyndid, v. dwindled away, vanished, 342.

table, n. table, 332.
take, v. take, 168; taken, 297; *toke,* took, betook (him-
        self), 313; *token,* taken, 57.
tale, n. rumour, 102, 109.
talent, n. desire, 176.
talkes, v. talks, 177.
tecche, n. stain, 85.
teches, v. teaches, 34.
tell, v. tell, 114; *tolde,* told, 31, 36; *tolden,* told,
        109.
temple(s), n. temple(s), heathen place(s) of worship,
        5, 15, 28.
temyd, v. were controlled by, subjugated by, appertain-
        ed to, 15.

tene, n. sorrow, pain, suffering, 331.
teres, n. tears, 314, 332.
tethe, n. teeth, 297.
thar, *ther*, adv. there, 3, 94, 262.
that, pron. who, 74.
the, þe, þi, def. art. the, 34, 89, 111, etc.; pron. thee, 276, 326.
then, conj. then, 177.
thenke, *thynkes*, v. think(s), 224, 259.
thi, þi, pron. thy, thine, 124, 185, 193, etc.
thykke, adj. thick, 47.
this, þis, adj. this, 11, 33, 98.
thre, adj. three, 49.
threnen, n. thrice, 210.
thrid, adj. third, 31.
thryuandly, adv. vigorously, 47.
throghe, prep. through; *thurghe*, þurghe, prep. through, 123, 192.
throghe, n. tomb, 47.
til(l), prep. until, 12, 136, 313.
tyme, n. time, 5, 15, 24, etc.
tithynges, n. tidings, news, 57.
title, n. name, 28; inscription, 102.
to, prep. to, 14, 15, 20, etc.; part. 6, 39, 40, etc.; *to geder*, adv. together, 350.
token, n. token, sign, 102; see *take*.
toles, n. tools, 40.
tome, n. opportunity, 313.
to-rent, v. torn in pieces, 164.
toumbe, n. tomb, 46, 57, 139.
toun, n. town, 5, 26, 34.
toward, prep. toward, 161.
trew, abs. adj. true, righteous men, 336.
Triapolitan(es), n. neologism, apparently indicates three most important areas: York, Canterbury, London, 31, 36.
trillyd, .v. flowed in a slender stream, 322.
Troie, *Troye*, *Troy*, n. here New Troy, i.e. London, 25, 211, 246.

tronyd, v. throned, 255.
troubull, n. trouble, disturbance, 109.
trouthe, n. truth, 13, 184, 268.
trowid, v. believed, 204, 255.
tulkes, n. men, 109.
turnes, *turnyd*, v. turns, changed, 15, 177.
twayne, n. two, 32; *two*, adj. two, 91.

þ*agh(e)*, þ*of*, conj. although, 122, 243, 244, etc.
þ*ai*, pron. they, 9, 43, 45, etc.
þ*at*, conj. that, 8, 36, 42, etc.; dem. pron, 19, 25,
     36, etc.
þ*e*, see *the*.
þ*en*, adv. then, 11, 13, 73, etc.; dem. pron. than, 230,
     270; conj. 137, 165, 320, etc.
þ*er*, adv. there, 39, 52, 53, etc.; þ*ere as*, adv. there
     where, 167; þ*erafter*, adv. afterwards, 189;
     þ*erinne*, adv. at that time, 27; þ*erof*, adv. from
     that, 339; þ*eron*, adv. on it, 79; þ*eroute*, adv.
     out of it, 291; þ*er-till*, adv. to it, 69; þ*er-to*,
     adv. to it, 59, 70.
þ*es*, adj. these, 155, 317.
þ*ider*, adv. thither, there, 58, 63, 64; þ*iderwarde(s)*,
     adv. thitherward, there, 61, 116.
þ*ou*, pron. thou, 159, 179, 181, etc.
þ*ousand*, adj. thousand, 210.
þ*ritty*, adj. thirty, 210.
þ*us*, adv. thus, 96, 99, 179, etc.

vayles, v. avails, 348.
vayne, adj. vain, 348.
vche, adj. each, 204, 275, 348; *vschon*, each on (?), 93.
verray, adj. precise, 53; *verrayly*, adv. truly, 174.
vertue(s), n. virtue, efficacy, 174, 286.
vghten, n. early morning before dawn, 118.
vigures, n. figures, 53.
visite, v. to visit, inspect, 108.
vison, n. vision, true dream, 121.
vnchaungit, adj. unchanged, 95.
vnclosid, v. opened, unlocked, 140.

vnder, adj. under, 70, 166, 203, etc.
vnhapnest, adj. most miserable, unfortunate, 198.
vnknawen, adj. unknown, 147.
vnlouke, v. to unlock, 67, 162.
vnpreste, adj. unready, not in service, 255.
vnsaȝt, adj. hostile, 8.
vnskathely, abs. adj. harmless, 278.
vnsparid, adj. limitless, 335.
vnwemmyd, adj. immaculate, 96, 266; *wemles*, spotless, 85.
vnworthi, adj. unworthy, 122.
vouche safe, v. vouchsafe, bestow, 121.
vp, adv. up, 118, 178, 349; *vpon*, on, 175, 202, 290.
vs, pron. us, 185, 212, 294.
vset, vsit, vsyt, v. used, 187, 200, 270.

waggyd, v. wagged, shook (his head), 281.
wakenyd, v. aroused, stirred up, 218.
wale, v. choose, in abundance, 73.
Wales, n. Wales, 9.
walon, v. swarmed, 64.
wan, v. won, 301.
warpyd, v. cast, 321.
was, see *be*.
water, n. water, 316, 329, 333.
we, pron. we, 155, 156, 169, etc.
wede(s), n. clothes, 77, 85, 96.
wegge, weghe, n. man, 96, 186; *wehes*, men, 73.
weldes, v. wields, rules, 161.
wele, comp. adv. well, 183; *wele dede*, adj. good deeds, 301; *for wothe ne wele*, for better or worse, 233; *welneghe*, adv. wellnigh, almost all, 119.
wemles, adv. spotless, 85.
wenten, v. went, 69.
wepand, v. weeping, 122; *wepid, wepyd*, v. wept, 220, 310.
were, see *be*.
weres, v. wears, 222.
werke, worke, n. work, 61; *werke men*, workmen, 69; *New Werke*, a section of St. Paul's, 38; *wyrke, worche*, v. work, 39.
werre, n. war, 215.

weshe, v. wash, 333.

wete, n. wet; *wete of eghen*, tears, 321.

wyʒt, adj. strong, able, 69.

wille, n. will, desire, 226.

wynter, n. winter, i.e. years, 230.

wise, n. manner, 77, 132, 229.

wyt, with, wyth, conj. with, 40, 48, 51, etc.; prep. with, 55, 62, 69, etc.; *wytin(ne), in wyt*, prep. within, 64, 68, 75; *wyt outen*, prep. without, 85.

witere, v. inform, make clear, 185.

witerly, adv. certainly, undoubtedly, 183.

wold, v. would, 68.

wonder, wondres, n. wonder(s), marvel(s), 57, 73, 93.

wonnes, v. dwells, 279.

wontyd, v. wanted, lacked, 208.

woo, n. woe, sympathy, 310.

worde(s), n. word(s), 56, 176, 191, etc.

worlde, n. world, 64, 186, 218.

wormes, n. worms, 262.

worth, v. subjunctive, expressing a wish for something to happen, 258; *blessid þou worth*, thou shalt be blessed, 340; *worthyn*, v. attained, 330.

wos, see *be*.

wost, wot, v. know, 183, 185.

wothe, n. harm, anger; *wothe ne wele*, for better or worse, 233.

wrakeful, adj. vengeful, 215.

wrange, adj. wrong, unjust, 236; n. wrong, injustice, 243.

wrath(e), n. anger, 233.

writtes, n. writing, book, 277.

wroght(es), v. made, worked, 226, 274; *wroghtyn*, made, behaved, 301.